Life as a Colonist

by Bob Rybak

illustrated by Susan Kropa

FS-10139 Life as a Colonist
All rights reserved–Printed in the U.S.A.
Copyright © 1994 Frank Schaffer Publications, Inc.
23740 Hawthorne Blvd.
Torrance, CA 90505

TABLE OF CONTENTS

INTRODUCTION

The World's Best Teacher

I have found the very best teacher in the world. It is not a person nor a book. It is personal experience. No matter how many times I tell my students something or warn them or advise them or preach to them, it simply does not sink in and become meaningful until they have literally learned it for themselves by some kind of experience. When they do, it as though the sky opened up and revealed a great mystery. At that moment, learning often compounds itself as students synthesize what they have just learned with other things they know. I would be willing to wager that most teachers have had the same experience.

The fact is most of us learn best that way. I know I had to touch the hot stove to understand the warnings of my parents. Experience works best because we all have the ability to internalize new information with already learned material and develop new ideas. I have often thought how terrific it would be to jump into a time machine and live the experiences of 50, 100, or 300 years ago. Living the way others did would enrich our foundation of experiences and enable us to compound them into new ideas.

Unfortunately, when students study history, they cannot go back and experience what it was like. They have to read about it or listen to someone talk about it, or if they are really lucky they might go on a field trip and see something related to it. My experience as a teacher has been that things do not really sink in if students only read or listen, and field trips are often limited.

As a consequence of these limited resources, the study of history often develops into a study of historical events and people. Students dutifully (or sometimes begrudgingly) learn the facts as they move chronologically forward in their historical studies.

What I want for my students is more than the read-it-and-listen-to-me-talk-about-it approach to history. I want them to experience the time machine method of learning history. Since I do not have a time machine, I can only provide the next best thing: a plan which allows students to experience life as others have and use those experiences to reflect on what they are living today so that they can create new ideas and perspectives. This plan neatly sums up the intent of this book.

Bridging the Gap

The colonial experience began over 300 years ago. For students who think last summer's most popular music is ancient history, 300 years is nearly an unbridgable chasm. Just the daily routine of the colonists is as foreign to my students as a packaging label written in another language. Yet it was the colonial experience that in many ways has determined the way Americans live and think today. The only way to bridge that gap is by getting students to live some of the experiences that the colonists lived and then have them reflect on those experiences and internalize them. For that to happen two things are needed. First, students need to have relevant experiences that parallel the everyday experiences of the colonists. Second, they need supplementary information that clearly explains what the colonial experience was like. *Life as a Colonist* does both of these things.

This book is set up to provide you, the teacher, with some information not typically found in a history book. The material focuses on the daily living of a colonist. Their homes, their diet, marriages, children, education, fun and games, and how they did their work are only a few of the facets covered in this book. Although this material does not completely replace the historical events students need to learn, all of it is relevant and worthwhile. Just telling them this information, however, misses the point. Students need to experience it as closely as possible and relate it to their own lives.

The activities provided in each chapter are designed to do just that. Within each chapter are student activities that provide them with the experience they need to put one and one together. The first "one" is the colonial experience. The second "one" is their own experience, and hopefully the "two" that they arrive at will be a new perspective.

How to Use This Book

Life as a Colonist is divided into 10 chapters, each one being one aspect of colonial living. Taken as a whole they help to create a picture of the colonial experience. Each of the 10 chapters is divided into smaller units. For example, the chapter on the homes of the colonists is divided into units on 1) the colonists' first shelter, 2) how colonists improved their homes, 3) house size, 4) how they furnished their homes, and 5) the building tools they used. Each unit has information specifically selected to be passed on to students along with activities that allow students to interact with the information.

There is no special formula to follow when integrating the information with the activities. You can provide the activity as a lead-in to a concept or first provide the information and follow it up with an activity. You are free to change the activities to fit your classroom circumstances.

Following the 10 chapters is a set of resource materials and an index to the activities. The resource material includes a list of books, both fiction and nonfiction, that students can use to supplement their study of the colonial era. Also included are two teacher resources: a list of computer programs on the colonial era and a list of print resources for teachers. The index provides a quick reference to all activities. It also provides a list of subjects and skills to which each activity relates. In developing your plans, therefore, you will be able to more easily integrate the study of the colonial period with other subjects.

Fitting the Curriculum

Accountability, one of the more dominating movements today in education, has the undesirable side effect of constricting the experiences we provide students in the classroom. This happens because we as teachers are compelled to design our teaching to facilitate clear evaluation of all material covered. As a consequence, activities that do not conform to easily graded paper and pencil evaluation methods often are seen as enrichment (i.e., extra stuff for which we do not have time). Teaching students the total colonial experience is not a frill. It is not enrichment. It is as important as all the dates and events they commit to memory.

Evaluating what students learn from this kind of material can be done in valid and even traditional ways. The most common is to have them write a reaction paper to an activity. If students are unfamiliar with this form of evaluation, then they need some guidelines. For example, they will need to know what the objective of the writing is. They will need to understand that they must reflect on what they learned from the activity and be able to explain how it relates to the colonial experience and their own lives.

Many of the activities are designed to have students interact with one another and then report back to the class. Both phases can become part of the evaluation process. Teachers can observe the discussion and note contributions as well as listen and grade the final presentation.

Life as a Colonist provides teachers with the opportunity to link students to an entirely different era in American history and allows them to learn lessons that are unimaginable without a time machine.

CHAPTER ONE

The Home of the Colonist

Early Colonists

When one thinks of a typical colonial home, the image that comes to mind is a wooden frame, salt-box style house. That, however, is only one style of house developed by colonists, and that style was fairly advanced compared to the types of homes built by the earliest colonists. In roughly 170 years of American colonialism, two things affected the style and furnishing of houses–time and location. The dwellings of the earliest colonists were in no way similar to the sturdy mansions that existed in America 125 years after the settlement of Jamestown (1607).

The early colonists were trailblazers. They arrived in America with very little and had to use the materials that were available to construct a dwelling that would shelter their families from the climate. In Virginia, and specifically Jamestown, records indicate that tents were erected. These tents were probably constructed of cloth that would have been used to replace damaged sails had they been torn or otherwise destroyed during the voyage to America. Tents would have worked in this warmer climate until sturdier wooden housing could have been constructed. The settlers also made shelters constructed of sticks, thatch, and mud daub often in a lean-to fashion on the side of a hill. These shelters were called English wigwams.

In some early New England colonies the colonists may have relied on caves or even holes covered with sails for shelter. In Plymouth it is surmised that the first homes were very small, crude huts that provided shelter from the elements. Log cabins as we know them were totally unheard of until the Finnish and Swedish settlers arrived in the 1640s. That style of house construction was eventually favored by later pioneers but was unused by the earliest colonists.

ACTIVITY   *Designing a House*

This activity allows students to go through the same reasoning process that colonists would have gone through in selecting a location and the materials needed for their first shelter. It then has them apply those criteria to their own environment. The ideal format for this activity is cooperative grouping of two to three students. If team members live close to one another, they will find it easier to share ideas because their neighborhoods (and frame of reference) are the same.

1. Teams should compose lists of likely sheltering places in their neighborhoods. Colonists were always mindful of where they located their houses. They needed to be safe from the elements (e.g., away from low-lying places that might flood) yet able to defend their homes. Teams will need to list criteria colonists would have had and apply those criteria in selecting their sites.

2. Teams should make up lists of materials found in their communities or neighborhoods that could be used to create simply constructed, sturdy shelters. Regardless of where students live, in a rural or suburban setting, they have the opportunity to closely simulate the kind of process the early colonists used. Have them take a look at the kinds of natural material their environment affords. They should notice the kinds of trees that grow and evaluate whether these trees are suitable for shelter. They should note whether the soil has rocks that could be used in home construction. They may even need to dig to find out what type of soil is available for construction. (For example, is clay available for mud daubing?)

If your students live in an urban or well-developed suburban community, natural locations and materials may not be readily available, but they can still apply the criteria to their neighborhood environment. As a follow-up, students will be able to relate how the urban setting presents many of the same problems to the homeless that the wilderness presented to the colonists.

3. Teams will present four items to the class.

- They must develop lists of possible materials and locations for the homes.
- They need to provide explanations of how the materials would be used to make simple dwellings.
- The teams will draw diagrams illustrating their constructions.
- They will design maps identifying the locations. All of this information will be used to present the team's ideas and conclusions to the rest of the class.

How Colonists Improved Their Homes

The early colonists soon abandoned their first shelters in favor of new and improved varieties. Safety was utmost on the mind of the colonist. Thatch roofs were found to be very susceptible to fire. They were replaced by clapboard roofs and walls. The first chimneys were also a fire hazard. Surprisingly, most of them were made out of logs that were coated with clay. By 1631 (only 10 years after the founding of Plymouth), this style of chimney was banned in the Massachusetts Bay Colony because of the great fire hazard it presented. Colonists eventually came to rely on other natural materials. Lime for making mortar was found in the oyster shell beds of the North and in natural formations throughout the southern colonies. Clay for making brick as well as stone was found in abundance throughout New England.

A colonist, therefore, made the building of a second more permanent and safer structure a primary concern once he and his family felt established in their new environment. It was during this middle colonial time period that the salt-box style house with its clapboard design became popular. The typical colonial home evolved over the years. As the family grew, additions were built. Typically, when more space was needed, the back roof was extended to cover a lean-to style addition. This created a home style known as the salt-box home. Salt-box homes used clapboard roofs.

In many colonies the wealth of clay allowed brick to be styled, and some homes were made of this safer and more durable material. Brick, of course, was reserved for the wealthier of the colonists. Stone was used by the commoner who used the same stones he found while cleaning his field to fashion chimneys and walls.

ACTIVITY   *Evaluating House Design*

This activity is an extension of the previous activity. Its purpose is to get students to consider the advantages and disadvantages of the homes they constructed and to suggest improvements. Eventually the conclusions that students reach will form a basis for understanding improvements colonists made to their own homes.

After each team has had the chance to present its plan for a house and has had a chance to listen to all other plans, have members continue working as a team to list advantages and disadvantages of materials, location, and construction of the dwellings they have designed. Students should be instructed to focus on several items in their evaluation including durability of the materials, quickness with which their dwelling could be constructed, and most important, safety of the dwelling as it is used every day. The activity sheet entitled "Making Necessary Changes" provides a guide for students as they progress in their evaluation and planning.

Finally, each team is to recommend changes in design for house construction and plan on reporting its decisions to the class. The findings of the students can be condensed into a class list that should help them understand how colonists changed their house designs to accommodate safety and a growing family.

Name _____

Making Necessary Changes

Background

When colonists arrived in America, shelter was their first consideration. Their first houses were put together quickly but needed to be sturdy enough to withstand the elements. In time, each colonial family worked to improve its home to accommodate a growing family and to make it safer and generally more livable. This may have meant adding to the existing structure, replacing parts of the home with fire-safe materials, reinforcing the existing structure with more durable materials, or redesigning a portion of the house to make it more weatherproof. In some cases entirely new homes were built in better locations.

The Goal

It is the goal of your team to collaborate to improve the shelter you originally designed. Changes should be based on the criteria mentioned above. These criteria should include the following:

1. providing for a larger number of family members
2. making your home fire safe
3. making your home more durable so that it will not deteriorate
4. improving your home so that it is more weatherproof (warmer in the winter or cooler in the summer, drier during rains)

Evaluating the Existing Design

Begin by evaluating the house you originally designed. Using the chart on the following page, focus on each of the following criteria and list the advantages and disadvantages of your house design. For example, if your team designed its house with a stone chimney, you should list that under "Advantages." On the other hand, if it designed your roof to be made of thatch, then list it as a fire hazard under "Disadvantages."

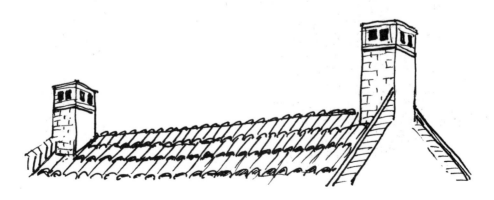

Name _____

Design Evaluation

ADVANTAGES   **DISADVANTAGES**

_____   _____
_____   _____
_____   _____
_____   _____
_____   _____
_____   _____
_____   _____

Deciding on Changes

Once you have listed all advantages and disadvantages, you will be better able to decide what needs to be changed. In the first column list the things that you think need to be changed, and in the second column explain what you would do to change them.

WHAT NEEDS TO BE CHANGED   **HOW TO CHANGE IT**

_____   _____
_____   _____
_____   _____
_____   _____
_____   _____
_____   _____

House Size

Because the first houses were little more than huts, one would think that the later, more permanent homes of the colonists would be contrastingly roomier and larger. This, however, was not the case. Although none of those first homes exists today, several of the second dwellings still exist. It would be difficult to classify all colonial homes of this second generation as fitting one size and design. Nonetheless, by today's standards they all seem modest in size. In Plymouth, for example, the homes were single-bay houses of about one-and-a-half stories. The living space may not have been divided at all. The single room was called the "hall." In it all the cooking, sleeping, and living took place. A typical house would measure 15 to 20 feet per side giving a maximum living area of 400 square feet in the hall.

A loft or chamber existed overhead as the half-story of these houses. One could not stand erect in it. It was accessed by a ladder or steep staircase built against the chimney. The loft was not as practical as today's second story rooms, but it was used as a sleeping area as well as for storage.

ACTIVITY   *Measuring Living Space 1*

This activity is designed to allow students to contrast the amount of living space the colonists had with their own living space. Begin by demonstrating the math used to compute square footage of living space. Measure the classroom's width and length and multiply the two for square footage area.

Assign students the job of measuring the rooms of their houses or apartments. You can have them do the multiplying at home or just bring in the measurements and do the math in class. For students with very large homes, you may want to limit the assignment to the kitchen, a bedroom, and the family or living room to simulate the primary colonial living areas.

These numbers can then be contrasted with the 336 square feet of living space in the Churchill, Sparrow, or Howland colonial homes which are still standing today. You may want to go out on the playground and mark off the 16' x 21' area that represents one of these houses. Use some of the students' own figures to create their living spaces. Putting students at the corners is an easy way to mark off the area. You can have these students hold string around the perimeter for an even better visual representation.

It is difficult to estimate how much actual living space each colonial family would have had in one of the typical single-bay homes that made up the second generation of houses. This is so because colonial families differed in size according to whether they were just starting out (a husband, wife, and one child), well developed (husband, wife, and five children), or older (husband and wife with children grown and gone). According to a 1689 census for Bristol, Rhode Island, however, the average was around six family members per household. Bristol appears to be an accurate representative case of what households were like in colonial New England. Given this number of six, then, the following activity will help students better visualize what it was like to live in the amount of space available in a modest colonial house.

ACTIVITY *Measuring Living Space 2*

Begin by demonstrating the process used to determine average square feet of living space per person. Do this by using the square footage from the classroom and divide that number by the number of students (plus the teacher) to determine how much living space each person has in the room.

Using the averages of 400 square feet of living space per single-bay house and six people per household, have students calculate the amount of living space available in one of these homes. The number should be about 67 square feet per person, not counting the loft/sleeping area. Students can also experiment with different family sizes to get different per-person ratios for the purpose of contrast.

To give students an idea of the size of 67 square feet of living space, tape off a 6' 8" x 10' area in the classroom. Give students time to walk around in this area. Leave it marked off for a week and have them take turns "living" in it. To reinforce the idea of how little space this is, ask students how many of their possessions they could fit into this area. Remind them that all furniture, pots, pans, and housewares had to fit into a single home, further reducing personal space by as much as 15 square feet.

Finally, have students determine the amount of living space per person for their own families using the numbers they obtained by measuring their own homes. Create a bulletin board chart that lists student names and per-person living space in their homes with the 67 square feet of the average colonial home listed first.

Colonial House Floor Plan

It would be difficult to identify one style of housing during the Colonial Period in America. This is because such diverse people came to America, each with a style of housing from the homeland that he or she sought to imitate. In the North the English colonists required as snug and warm a house as possible. Houses were, therefore, smaller with a fireplace in the center of the hall. In some cases the hall was divided into two rooms. This was done by erecting a wall as a partition to create an "inner room." This room had many possible functions. It could be used as a work room or a master bedroom for the parents with the children occupying the loft.

Colonial architecture continued evolving into the eighteenth century. The English colonists began building houses with several main rooms downstairs and partitioned lofts upstairs or added a second story. The first extra room often became a "parlor" or sitting room and obviously represented a greater establishment and greater wealth in the New World. In cities where well-to-do merchants had been living for several generations, the houses were much greater in size and more elaborate in design.

The Dutch who settled in New York developed houses that reflected their practical-minded nature. Several building materials might be used in one house. Dormers were added for space. Gambrel roofs (see illustration below) were developed because of the extra space they allowed the family.

Although the earliest southern homes were constructed of wood, the southern colonists adopted brick as their building material of choice as soon as brick-making became common. Southern homes tended to be long and narrow (20' x 40') with fireplaces at each end. The warmer climate allowed colonists to build more spacious houses since heating them was not a year-round primary concern. In fact, since the summers were so hot, it was better to have the kitchen with its cooking fireplace somewhat separated from the eating area.

Colonial Furnishings

What would you expect to see in any colonial house? Students can answer that question (and *should* as a lead-in to this lesson) by looking at their own homes. The furnishings of a colonial home served the same purposes as today's modern furnishings. Chief among these was a heat source. Today we have furnaces and ovens. The colonists combined the two into the single most important item in any home, the fireplace.

In the North this dual-function fireplace was a lifeline during the bitterly cold winters. A typical fireplace in a small single-bay home would be 8 to 10 feet wide and as high as 4 feet. Considering overall size, the house was rather large. Its size, however, was an indication of its importance. But, despite its size, the loft area and corners of the house were still chilly. In the North these fireplaces were not placed, as they often are today, on a wall. They were wholly inside the hall and sometimes in the very center of the room so that as much heat as possible would be kept in the house. In the South, where winters were mild and summers could be unbearably hot, fireplaces were located on an outside wall.

All these fireplaces required great amounts of wood and much care. One fireplace could easily burn 15 to 20 cords of wood a year (each cord is a pile of wood measuring 4' x 4' x 18'). Cleaning the chimney was a heavy chore that was done primarily with a broom. On occasion, a chicken was dropped down the chimney to clean the harder-to-reach places with its wildly beating wings.

The primary consideration when choosing furniture was economy of space. The single most important large furnishing was a chest. Most early colonial homes had little storage space, and it was unheard of to have closets. A chest served not only as storage but also as a seat or table. When a table did exist, it, too, was constructed to economize space. Trestle tables were used because they could be taken apart and stored against a wall when not in use. These were called *board tables* rather than dining tables, from which we get the expression "room and *board*." There were few chairs, although stools were common. If a chair did exist, it was reserved for the master of the house or an older person (thus the word *chairman*). Dinnerware was often stored on or in a chest. Evidence suggests that in some households members ate while standing.

Beds and bedsteads were also designed for economy of space. A flock bed was nothing more than a bag stuffed with cornhusks, rags, or anything that might make a soft mattress. It could be rolled up and stored when not in use. Feather beds were similar but contained only feathers and represented wealth. Some bedsteads were made from lengths of cord laced back and forth across a wooden frame. Sometimes these frames were attached to the wall with leather hinges so they could be closed up in the morning to be out of the way. The trundle bed was another space saver that allowed one bed to be stored under the frame of a larger bedstead.

Bed clothing was common and included sheets, covers, pillows, pillowcases, coverlets, and curtains (for those wealthy enough to have curtained bedsteads). Warming pans, boxes made of metal that contained hot coals, were also found in the sleeping area. They were used for warmth on especially cold nights. Rugs were included in a number of inventories, although they would not have been used as floor coverings but as wall, window, or bed coverings.

Because the hall was the center of activity for most chores, the tools of those chores were also noticeable. All the cooking utensils (discussed more extensively in Chapter 3) were located close to the fireplace. There was generally a spinning wheel in the hall. Axes, guns, tools for making shot, powder horns, mallets, saws, chisels, carding brushes, knives, hoes, fishing tackle, assorted wooden bowls, barrels, butter churns, lengths of rope, and a broom might all occupy some space in the hall. Oftentimes the floorboards of the loft were not permanently attached to the joists so they would be removable. In this way large, heavy items could be more easily hauled up to the loft area.

Eventually a family would build a shed to help store these items. As houses increased in size over the years, more and more storage and living space became available. These first colonial homes, however, were quite crowded.

ACTIVITY *Developing a Floor Plan*

The student page entitled "A Colonial Floor Plan" gives students the opportunity to decide how they would arrange a colonial home's furnishings to maximize space. Students can use the activity sheet to plan the furnishings they want to include for their families. You may want to require certain furnishings. Then have them design floor plans on the reproducible graph paper (page 13) that is made to a scale of 1/2" to the foot. When students are finished, they should prepare short papers in which they explain how some of the above items would be stored and how some of the furnishings on their floor plans would be used in more than one way. Their final plans and papers can be presented in small groups or to the class.

A Colonial Floor Plan

A colonial family with average means lived in a modest-sized house. In New England today there still exist houses built during colonial times. Their halls measure 16' x 21' with a loft for storage. This space had to accommodate an average of five or six family members and all their furnishings. Your job is to design a floor plan for such a family. Use the planning sheet below to guide you in this process. Then draw a floor plan on the graph paper to show what it would look like.

1. How large will your family be?　　five members　　six members

2. What are the ages of your family members?

　　____　　____　　____　　____　　____　　____

3. Is your home to be built in the northern or southern colonies?_____

_____

4. Where will you place your fireplace and what size will it be?

placement　_____　　size _____

5. How many of each of the following furnishings will you have?

chests (2' x 4')	_____	butter churn (18" round)	_____
chairs (18" x 18")	_____	trestle table (3' x 6')	_____
stools (1' round)	_____	barrels (18" round)	_____
beds (3' x 6')	_____	spinning wheel (2' x 3')	_____
bedsteads (4' x 7')	_____		

6. Keep these basic rules in mind as you plan:

   a. You must have at least one chest and two barrels in your household and a sleeping place for everyone.

   b. You must have something on which to eat.

   c. Each adult must have one seat.

   d. When possible use an item for more than one purpose.

   e. Use circles and rectangles to represent the furnishings, but draw them to scale.

13

FS-10139 Life as a Colonist

Colonial Tools

The colonist, whether just stepping off the boat in 1607 or living in the eighteenth century as a fourth generation descendant, needed the same basic tools and utensils to get by on a daily basis. Although our lives have changed dramatically in the past 100 years, the life of a colonist between the early 1600s and 1700s changed relatively little. As a consequence, his or her day-to-day equipment changed little as well.

The man of the household needed carpentry tools of all sorts. The primary one was the axe, the all-purpose tool that every colonial family had to have. It was used to clear trees, shape furniture, cut firewood, fashion snares, and build houses. Axes came in all sizes and shapes depending on their use and origin. *Felling axes* with their v-shaped cutting edges were used to fell trees and chop them into pieces. *Broad axes* had chisel-type edges and were used for hewing round logs into square beams. A hatchet with a smaller head and handle provided the colonist a hand hatchet which he could use with greater dexterity.

As master carpenters began to arrive in the New World, the tools became more specialized. A *froe* and *maul* were used to split wood into shingles and clapboards. *Adzes* with long handles helped to shape and smooth beams while the short-handled adzes could be used to shape small scoops and other wooden implements. Hammers with metal heads were very rare because nails were a rarity. Wooden mallets or mauls were used to pound chisels and wooden pegs in making furniture. The drawknife was used in all regions of the colonies. This tool helped form rounded pieces such as stool legs and handles; it was also used to taper shingles and trim floorboards.

The saw also held a place of importance in the gallery of colonial tools. *Open pit saws* were designed to be used by two men who would saw a slice out of a beam to be used as a plank in the floor or on the side of a house. The beam straddled a pit with one man atop the pit and the other in it. This arrangement gave them the up-and-down room they needed to saw the planks out of the beam. Open saws were similar to modern hand saws except the handles were more like those of a knife. These saws were common and enabled one person to do a variety of tasks.

If anyone has ever walked into an old barn and looked at some of the tools hanging on the walls or resting on the floor, he or she has probably asked the question, "For what was this thing used?" The colonists had many tools they used for dozens of different occasions. Some of these tools are easily identifiable while others could be puzzled over for days and never understood.

The activity sheet entitled "For What Was This Thing Used?" will give students an opportunity to match pictures of tools with descriptions of how they were used and for what. Most of the tools pictured would date anywhere from 1607 to 1770. They are the tools used mostly by men for building, shaping, planting, cultivating, and harvesting. (See Chapter 3 for a similar exercise that focuses attention on cooking and eating implements and Chapter 4 for one that focuses on tools used by women in their daily lives.)

It must be emphasized to students that people of the colonies became more and more resourceful as time passed. They changed and adapted tools to fit the jobs. Some of these adaptations caught on, and the "antiques" of their inventiveness are still used today.

Below is the answer key to the activity. You will need to reproduce both the clue page and the tool drawing page. By no means is this meant to be a complete portrayal of colonial tools; it is only a sampling. Missing are tools that would be instantly identified like saws and scythes.

Answers to "For What Was This Thing Used?"   Pages 16 and 17

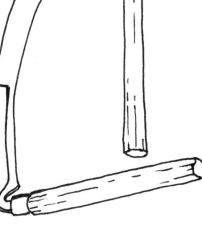

1. e hand adze
2. g drawknife
3. j bog root cutter
4. c broad axe
5. h ring dog

6. d dog
7. i spud
8. a hay crook
9. f froe
10. b nail header

Below are a few more tools you may want to present to the class.

maul—took the place of the hammer and
        was used to pound wooden pegs and
        froes

hay knife—cut a portion of hay out of a
        haystack

goose poke—placed on a goose's neck to
        keep it from getting through
        a fence

Name _____

"For What Was This Thing Used?"

Directions: Match the descriptions found on this page to the pictures of tools on the next page by writing the name of the tool on the blank beneath the picture.

a. This tool was used during harvesting to separate a portion of the hay so it could be easily cut with a reaping hook or scythe. It was called a *hay crook*.

b. This tool was used in nail making. After the nail had been tapered and cut, it was placed into this tool so that the head could be pounded into it. It was called a *nail header*.

c. This very early colonial axe was used to hew or chisel round logs into square beams. It was called the *broad axe*.

d. Getting a round log to lie still when trying to hew it square was not easy. This tool held a log in place so it could be squared. It was called a *dog*.

e. This hand tool was used to hollow out bowls or other wooden objects. It was called the *hand adze*.

f. When colonists wanted to make wooden shingles or clapboards, they used this tool to slice a larger piece of wood by driving it down through the wood with a mallet. It was called the *froe*.

g. This tool was used to trim boards, taper shingles, and shape floorboards. The colonist placed the board or piece of wood in front of him and pulled the blade toward himself against the wood. It was called the *drawknife*.

h. When large logs had to be moved by only one or two people, this tool was used to help roll the logs. It was called the *ring dog*.

i. After a tree was felled, the bark had to be stripped. This tool was like a long chisel. The colonist would place the blade under the bark and pry and chisel to remove the bark. It was called the *spud*.

j. Cutting down the tree was only half the battle. When clearing fields and marshes, the stump and its roots also had to be removed. This tool was used to cut tree roots so that stumps could be removed. It was called a *bog root cutter*.

Name _____

Directions: Below the picture of each colonial tool, write its name.

1. _____	6. _____
2. _____	7. _____
3. _____	8. _____
4. _____	9. _____
5. _____	10. _____

CHAPTER TWO
Colonial Diet: Food and Drink

From the Old World to the New

To understand the diet of the first English settlers, it is important to understand the kind of diet they had developed in their native England. "Bland" would be the term by today's standards. Englanders of the seventeenth century were not vegetable eaters. As they saw it, these were foods fit for pigs and wildlife more than for humans. Furthermore, vegetables eaten raw were deemed unhealthy. The exceptions to this rule were root vegetables, herbs, and grains. Root vegetables such as carrots, onions, parsnips, turnips, and beets were staples of most pottages (stews cooked in pots). These vegetables were often cooked for an extremely long time resulting in a rather tasteless thick soup.

One vegetable, however, was clearly a favorite of the seventeenth century Englander and the early colonist. It was the pea. The pea was used in a variety of stews and as a separate vegetable. In fact, this familiar old nursery rhyme dates back well before the days of the early American colonies:

Pease porridge hot.
Pease porridge cold.
Pease porridge in the pot nine days old.

Some like it hot.
Some like it cold.
Some like it in the pot nine days old.

The colonists brought the pea to America but found it did not grow as well as they had hoped. Consequently, a substitute was needed and found in the form of the bean. Beans were one of the vegetables that the native Americans of the Northeast called "the three sisters." (The other two "sisters" were corn and squash.) There were many different varieties of beans including red kidney beans, white navy beans, and large lima beans. The colonists from Maine to Georgia adopted them all. When harvested, they could be used fresh, but the real value of most varieties of beans was their ability to be dried and preserved to last throughout the long winter and until the next harvest.

ACTIVITY *Bean Varieties*

Dried beans became a staple of every home whether in the northern, southern, or middle colonies. Beans today are found in abundance and variety in our supermarkets and grocery stores. The following activity is designed to allow students to experiment with the variety of beans still available to Americans.

Purpose:

To compare and contrast the growth rates and success of different bean varieties. To reinforce the use of the scientific process.

Materials:

3-7 clear plastic cups
3-7 different varieties of dried beans
paper towels
water
3-7 pots filled with native soil (not needed if seedlings can be planted outside)

Procedure:

1. Label each cup and pot with the name of one of the bean varieties you have available.
2. Soak the paper towels and stuff them into the clear plastic cups so that they loosely fill the cup.
3. Carefully place about four to five beans of each variety inside the appropriately labeled cups. Do this by placing the beans between the wet towel and the side of the cup so that the beans can be observed as they sprout.
4. Wet towels as necessary during the length of the experiment.
5. When the seedlings have sprouted, transplant them in pots filled with native soil or outside in a sunny location. Keep the soil moist until the seedlings are established.

 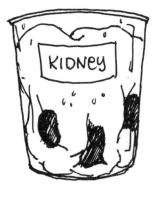 

Observations:

The goal of this activity is to compare the growth rates of different bean varieties. Students should keep a lab notebook during the experiment to reinforce the use of the scientific process. Included in this notebook should be the following:

–a statement of purpose for the experiment.

–the procedures that are planned.

–the aspects of the experiment that will be constants (e.g., soil, sunlight, water) and the variable (the different varieties of beans).

–daily observations of the sprouting, particularly noting which bean variety sprouts first and grows most quickly.

–daily observation of the growing and flowering once the seedling has been transplanted noting hardiness and ability to survive.

Note: Unless the beans are transplanted outdoors, pollination will likely not occur and the cycle will end after flowering. This makes for a natural end to the experiment.

Conclusions:

Students should focus their conclusions on what varieties of beans sprouted first, were most hardy, and generally would be the best to plant in the native soil of your area. Have them include in their conclusions anything they feel may have contributed to the success or failure of the experiment and what new information they want to learn about any of these varieties to expand their newly acquired knowledge about beans and their growth.

Colonial Link

Survival for the colonists depended on being able to grow food that could be preserved and grow enough of it to last until the next harvest. This experiment allows students to see that not all beans are alike. As a follow-up have them measure the root system of the different bean plants. One problem that New England colonists had was that the thin topsoil base was not good for any variety of plant that needed a deep root system. Have students conclude which bean variety would have been best in that category.

New England and even the middle colonies had a fairly short growing period. In their conclusions students can speculate which of the bean varieties would have best served these colonists based on growth rates.

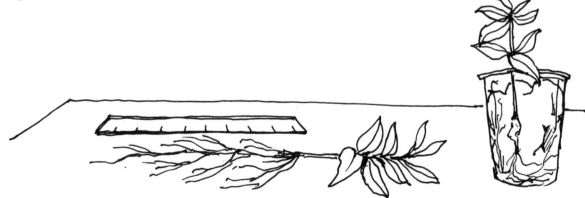

Corn–The Stalk of Life

In England the chief grains were wheat, oats, rye, and barley. The Pilgrims had a supply of these grains which they had intended to plant, but unfortunately (or fortunately depending on how one looks at it), much of their grain had either rotted or had become useless during the ill-timed voyage and subsequent wintering. In the spring an Algonquian named Squanto, who earlier in his life had been taken to England by British fishermen, taught the Pilgrims the rudiments of planting in this new world called *America*. The technique required the mounding of soil into a small hill into which was placed several seed kernels and some fertilizer. The fertilizer was a small herring-like fish such as a shad.

The corn was well-suited to the growing conditions of the northern area. First, it grew quickly allowing it to be harvested before the weather would freeze it. Second, it had a shallow root system that was well-suited to the thin topsoil of the New England region. In time, colonists were able to develop strains of wheat that were better suited to the climate and soil conditions of the area, but by that time corn had become a staple of the colonial dinner table.

Like the bean, corn could be dried and kept for an entire year. In its dried form it was pounded with a samp mortar. *Samp* was an Indian word for a porridge of cornmeal and water cooked over an open fire that became lumpy and thick as it cooked. A *samp mortar* was a tool made of a pounding implement (or mortar) attached to a young, flexible tree. The mortar was pulled down into a hollowed log with dried corn in it. The springiness of the tree automatically pulled the heavy mortar back making the tiring job of pounding the corn into meal easier. Soon, however, this mortar method of creating cornmeal was replaced by water-driven grist mills.

The Uses of Corn

Corn was found in almost every meal cooked by the early colonists. It was in the many varieties of breads that they made including johnnycake, spoon bread, corn oysters, and hush puppies. It was found in their meat stews as well as the vegetable dish they adapted from the Indians which is called *succotash* today. Breakfast porridge was made with cornmeal as was the dessert called Indian pudding. Corn on the cob was relished when fresh in August or early September. After the corn was dried, it could be crisped on hot ashes, pounded into smaller bits, and eaten as a treat. It was hard to imagine a day without corn for the seventeenth century colonist.

ACTIVITY   *Investigating Corn*

Before the seventeenth century, the word *corn* was used to refer to any grain that was used as the principal crop of a nation. Hence, wheat was the corn of England. To differentiate that meaning of corn from the Indian corn being used by the colonists, the word *maize* was used.

Today our domesticated corn is used in a variety of ways. Not only is it used as a raw food product, but it is also processed into a number of cereals and snacks.

By-products of corn such as corn oil, corn syrup, and corn starch are used in many ways. For example, corn oil is used in paints, cosmetics, and soaps. Other by-products of corn are used as packing material, fibers, adhesives, and in fabrics.

To increase awareness of how much corn is used in our daily lives, have students work in teams to do first-hand research. Teams can begin in the grocery store checking the packaging labels of as many foods as they can to see which foods contain corn in some form or other. These products can be organized according to the way the corn was used (e.g., raw corn items, items with corn syrup, and items with corn oil). Some teams may be able to contact paint, cosmetic, and other companies to develop their lists further.

The emphasis is to get students to do first-hand investigations (i.e., by talking to people). Give this project a generous time frame so that students can develop and follow through on their leads.

A bulletin board can be used to display the information teams are able to uncover.

Because corn and beans were so important to the colonial diet, you may want to incorporate some colonial cooking into the students' study. Cooking in the classroom is ideal but not often practical. Most of the recipes developed in this section only require a hot plate as a heat source. Toaster ovens or access to a cafeteria oven makes the Indian pudding recipe possible. If cooking in the classroom is not possible, making it an at-home activity still provides the experience for those involved. Having students bring in their creations and heating them will allow students to taste what our colonial ancestors ate on a regular basis.

Along these lines you may want to designate a day for colonial cooking (or tasting if students are cooking at home). Call it "Corn Day" since all of the recipes given use corn in one form or another.

General Cooking Notes

Keep in mind at all times that a colonist made do with what was available and spent much less time measuring amounts than people do today. The amounts listed below are guidelines. You will find the recipes rather forgiving. If you begin to cook several of these dishes, do not be afraid to cook with instinct. Check for doneness yourself and do not rely on the clock. Colonists surely did not.

Also, do not be afraid to make variations. By making two versions of the same basic recipe, students can taste the difference themselves and decide which they would make again if they were colonists.

Since colonists did not always have some ingredients. You may want to improvise as they would have. Some recipes call for sugar. Refined white sugar was not available in the seventeenth century as it is today. Colonists used any other sweeteners they could find. Molasses was very common as trade from the West Indies was well established soon after the Massachusetts Bay Colony was founded. You may want, however, to be careful with molasses; it has a rather strong taste. Honey and maple sugar were other sweeteners used in colonial days, and each added its own flavor to the recipe.

The colonist usually used white pepper, but black pepper does not seem to change the taste of the recipes. With black pepper being more coarsely ground, you may want to add a little more.

Succotash

This was undoubtedly one of the first recipes that the colonists learned from the native Americans. Known to the Indians as *sukquttahash,* this dish was both adopted and adapted by colonists to fit their tastes and means. It is made primarily of navy beans and corn. The navy beans were also called white pea beans resembling (at least in size) the peas that the colonists were used to eating in England. The corn was usually dried, although the recipe here uses a canned version for simplicity. The succotash recipe below was the winter variety that colonists ate more regularly. It is made of dried beans and corn. Modern succotash is made with fresh corn and lima beans. That is the colonial summer version.

The following recipe will make about 30 small, sample-sized servings.

Ingredients:

1 cup uncooked dried navy beans (white pea beans)
2 twelve-oz. cans sweet corn or 1-1/2 cups dried corn
1/4 cup margarine or butter (1/4 cup = 1/2 stick)
1-1/2 cups milk
1/4 cup flour (basic all purpose flour will do)
1/2–1 tsp. salt
1 tsp. sugar or other sweetener
pepper to taste

Procedure:

1. Put the beans and dried corn (optional) in cold water overnight to soften. Make sure water covers them.
2. The next day, boil the beans and dried corn. The boiling is really a simmering. Be careful of boiling over; the mixture tends to foam up. Figure one hour for the beans to cook and about 40 minutes for the dried corn. Note–Do NOT cook the corn if it is canned.
3. Melt the butter in a large pot. At the same time, mix the milk and flour. Whisk it for best results to eliminate lumps.
4. Mix the flour and milk mixture in with the butter and heat on medium–stirring continually until the mixture thickens.
5. Add the beans and corn (cooked or canned). Also add the sugar, salt, and pepper. Continue heating until it is warm but not boiling. Then serve.

Variations:

Colonists added many different things to this basic recipe including nuts (in season), onions, bacon, salt pork, and corned beef. Let students make suggestions and try them. Add these ingredients in step five. Be certain to determine whether any of these ingredients needs to be cooked before it is added to the recipe.

Johnnycake

Johnnycake is a derivation of the words *journey* and *cake*. It is a cornmeal based cake ideal for travel, whereby it got its original name *journey cake*. Eventually the *r* got lost in the pronunciation, and it was not long before an *h* was added to the spelling giving it its present-day misnomer.

The first johnnycake was strictly a corn bread attempt at making the breads the colonists relished back in England. One real important difference, however, made corn unsuitable for rising–it had no gluten. *Gluten* is a protein that gives raw dough its elasticity and holds in the CO_2 produced by yeasts. Thus, wheat bread with gluten will inflate (rise), but a corn dough mixture allows the CO_2 to escape, thus no rising.

Another characteristic of this first corn bread was its crumbly nature. Both of these "problems" were eventually solved by adding a little wheat or rye flour to the mixture, both of which have gluten. Although the rising was not as pronounced, the crumbly nature of the bread lessened. The recipe below is the "improved" version with wheat flour. You may, however, want to try out the more original johnnycake recipe by leaving out the wheat flour. When this recipe is complete, it represents what the Indians called *corn pone*.

Ingredients:

1 cup all purpose flour
a little over 1 cup cornmeal (white or yellow)
2 tsp. baking powder
2 tbs. sweetener (honey, molasses, or sugar)
1 tsp. salt
1 egg
3 tbs. melted butter or bacon drippings
1 cup milk

Procedure:

1. Mix the dry ingredients together in a separate bowl.
2. Blend the liquid ingredients in another bowl.
3. Combine liquid and dry ingredients in a few strokes; do not overdo it.
4. Place the batter in a greased skillet and cover it. Cover and cook it for about 30 minutes on low/medium heat. Check it for doneness occasionally making certain it is not burning on the bottom.
5. For individual servings, pour small portions onto a griddle and cook them like pancakes.

Variations:

Here again, you can add anything you like to the mixture. Make it hardy with nuts or cooked meats, make it dessert-like with raisins or dried fruits, or let students decide what to add.

Indian Pudding

The colonists loved their sweets. Molasses was the chief sweetening ingredient. In fact, when trading ships were late in getting to the ports, entire holidays (such as Thanksgiving) were postponed. Without access to molasses, colonists would use substitutes like honey or maple syrup. In the recipe below, the end product has a ginger snap taste. The consistency is not creamy like today's puddings; it is more like a porridge. Extra sugar may be added to taste.

Indian pudding would have better been named corn pudding because it was devised as a substitute for the traditional English puddings that required wheat flour. The English considered anything cold and sweet a dessert and anything hot and sweet a pudding. Thus, Indian pudding is meant to be a hot dessert. That would be the traditional way to serve it. American tastes for pudding run on the cold side. To break tradition even more, serve it with ice cream or whipped cream.

The following recipe is designed to make eight full servings. Half portions work fine in the classroom and eliminate waste which means the recipe will serve 16. Double the recipe and you will have plenty for tasting and leftovers for those who love the pudding. The doubling also requires students to exercise math skills. Let students read over the recipe and decide what utensils and containers they need.

Ingredients:

*4 cups milk	1 tsp. salt
1/3 cup cornmeal	1 tsp. ginger
3/4 cup molasses	1-2 tsp. cinnamon
1/4 cup (1/2 stick) butter	3 eggs

Procedure:

1. Pour the milk into the pot and scald it. Scalding occurs when little bubbles form along the side of the pot. *Do not allow the milk to boil.* Have someone keep watch.
2. Add cornmeal to the scalded milk a little at a time and stir it to prevent lumps. Add molasses and butter. Turn down the heat and stir occasionally until this mixture thickens.
3. While this mixture is heating, beat the eggs; add cinnamon, ginger, and salt. Stir or whisk frequently to prevent spices from settling.
4. Add the liquid mixture to the egg mixture and mix well.
5. Grease the baking or casserole dishes and add the mixture.
6. An option is to add raisins or apples to the mixture.
7. Cook for 1-1/2 to 2 hours.

---

* If you add apples, reduce the amount of milk by the number of cups of cut apples you use. (1 cup apples means you use only 3 cups milk.)

Chocolate morsels may be used, but the taste of the chocolate does not mix well with the pudding.

Hush Puppies

The South was also part of this colonial period, and the people of the South likewise adopted corn as a staple of their diet. North Carolina's climate especially lent itself to the growing of corn. The Southern variation of johnnycake was called the *hoe cake* or *ashcake*. The dough was made with cornmeal, salt, milk (or water), and lard or pork drippings. The stiff dough was molded into a flat cake and cooked on the farmer's hoe. Ashcake was the same except that the dough was wrapped in cabbage leaves and placed in hot ash.

The hush puppy developed as a favorite with the plentiful fish and seafood eaten by southerners. Many sources speculate that the name comes from the practice of saying "hush puppy" while throwing one of these delectables to the dogs to get them to stop whining while the food fried on the skillet.

The recipe below makes about 15 two-inch hush puppies. For an entire class, plan on having the students figure out how to double the ingredient amounts. Also have them read over the recipe in advance to figure out what utensils they will need.

Ingredients:

1 cup cornmeal
1 tsp. baking powder
1 tsp. salt
a pinch of pepper
1/2 tsp. of sugar (optional)
1 small, finely chopped onion (optional)
1/4 cup milk
1/4 cup water
1 egg
vegetable oil for frying

Procedure:

1. In a bowl, mix the cornmeal, baking powder, salt, pepper, sugar, and onion together.
2. Then beat together the milk, water, and egg.
3. Combine the liquid mixture with the dry ingredients and hand mix until smooth.
4. Pour the vegetable oil into a skillet about 1/4" deep and when the oil is hot, drop small mounds of the hush puppy mixture into the fat. Each mound should be about two inches.
5. Use a slotted spoon to turn hush puppies when they are brown on one side and to lift them out of the oil when they are done. Place them on a paper towel to drain and serve as soon as possible. You can also deep fat fry them if you have the equipment.

Variation:

Whereas the above recipe is authentic, modern hush puppies contain wheat flour making them moister. Add an extra 1/4 cup water or milk and you will get a moister dough mixture that is easier to handle but needs to fry more slowly.

Nutrition in the Colonies

For the first colonists keeping food in their stomachs was priority number one. No one asked the question, "Am I getting my daily minimum allowance of essential vitamins and minerals?" Even the colonists of the late seventeenth and eighteenth centuries did not concern themselves with nutrition as we do today. The colonial diet was determined by availability and custom. Summer and early autumn were times of plenty with fresh fruits and vegetables to supplement the always available supply of game, fish, and seafood. In early summer wild strawberries could be picked. Huckleberries, blackberries, and blueberries also supplemented colonists' diets. Persimmons, which were unknown in England, grew in such abundance that the vines broke from their weight. Cherry trees were brought from Europe and eventually cultivated. By late summer crops were being harvested. The corn and beans and squash were fresh as was any other grain that might have been planted such as rye or barley. Apples were ripe by September and provided fruit for an abundance of dishes. By the midseventeenth century every home had its own cottage garden of peas, onions, turnips, cabbage, and herbs. Consequently, the average meal during these seasons was considerably more nutritious than meals eaten during the winter or early spring. Nutrition in the South was even better because of a longer growing season and the abundance of wild plants which produced food longer than similar plants found in the North.

A Change in Diet

The colonists had to change from their traditional English eating habits when they came to America. It did not seem to have taken long to do so. In England the diet was heavy on carbohydrates and light on protein. That is because England could not inexpensively produce the livestock required to feed nobility, gentry, yeomen, and laboring poor alike. In New England the abundance of game, fish, and seafood caused most immigrants to experience a diet they had not known in England. Wild turkeys were said to travel in flocks of 400 or 500. Herring by the thousands invaded waterways in the spring, and the skies were darkened by ducks as they took flight.

Colonists experimented with all types of livestock in the New World including chickens, goats, sheep, cattle, and pigs. What the colonist learned was that hogs made the best type of livestock for their situation because they could root on their own and required little tending. Cows were prized for their milk but never slaughtered unless the colonist had plenty to spare. Goats and sheep required too much work and protection to be worthwhile. All of this led to a diet unusually high in protein compared to what colonists were used to in England.

Daily Fare

The difference between a late summer and a winter menu was more noticeable than the same difference is today. Today, importation of foods from South America and warm-weather states makes it possible to eat many fresh fruits and vegetables all winter long. That was not so for the northern colonists. The nutritious diet of autumn gave way to a nutrition poor winter diet. Foods that could be preserved were the entire bill of fare. They included dried corn and beans, salted pork and fish, and by the early eighteenth century corned (pickled) beef.

Consequently, the average daily winter menu was very standard. Breakfast consisted of a porridge and perhaps some bread. The main meal served between noon and three o'clock consisted of a stew containing dried vegetables and perhaps salted meat with johnnycake or later yeasted bread on the side. At times simple succotash might replace the stew. Supper was a lesser meal returning once again to a porridge. Any meal might include something sweet depending on the availability of sugar, molasses, honey, and maple syrup.

The colonial cook had little imagination in preparing foods, and consequently daily meals were often repetitious, bland, and low in nutrition. Porridges and stews dominated the dining table. This was not only a carryover from English cooking habits, but it was most practical. Food needed to be prepared in a way that required as little attention as possible since so much else needed to be done. Allowing a large pot attached to a crane to simmer all day over a fire suited this purpose. The resultant overcooking of the food, however, drained most of the nutrients out of the meal.

The colonial diet included little water. Colonists believed water was tied to illnesses and poor health–which it probably was with the standing waters that surrounded Jamestown. Consequently, they drank many other liquids such as beer, rum, cider, wine, and eventually milk. Nowadays water purification systems make drinking water safe, and nutritionists maintain that water is necessary for good health. Today, eight glasses of water are recommended daily.

Purpose:

To analyze the nutritional intake of an average colonist and compare it to the nutritional value of their own daily menu. Although students' data will focus on only one day's eating, it will provide a plausible snapshot of their eating habits for the comparison. This activity can be done individually or in cooperative groups.

Procedure:

1. Make copies of the page entitled "How Our Diets Compare" and "Nutritional Information Charts" to distribute to students.
2. On their own paper have students use the nutrition charts to make observations regarding the nutritional value of the meals eaten by colonists.
3. Have students keep a diary of their own eating habits for one day by creating a chart fashioned after the one entitled "What I Ate Today."
4. After that chart is completed, have students once again note observations regarding the nutritional value of the food they ate in one day's time.
5. Either have students prepare a paper that compares and contrasts the nutritional intake of a colonist to their own or have them discuss this issue in cooperative groups and prepare a summary report of the group's findings.

How Our Diets Compare

Below is a listing of everthing a colonist might have eaten in one day. It is more typical of a winter's meal. Use this information to analyze the nutrition a colonist received by referring to the "Nutritional Information Charts."

Breakfast	corn mush diluted with milk	1 serving
	molasses sweetener	2 tablespoons
	apple cider	2 cups
Dinner	succotash (stew made of corn, navy beans with salt pork)	2 servings
	johnny cake (corn bread)	2 servings
	molasses sweetener	2 tablespoons
	apple cider	2 cups
Supper	same as breakfast	same servings
Snacks	apple cider	1 cup
	johnny cake	1 serving

What I Ate Today

Create a chart fashioned after the one below. Fill it out by listing everything you eat in one day's time. Be sure to keep track of after school snacks, before bed snacks, glasses of water, as well as vitamins you may take. Gum does need not to be recorded but candy does. You can be the judge of how much food makes up a serving.

Meal	**Food**	**Servings**
Breakfast		
Dinner		
Supper		
Snacks (also including water and vitamins)		

Name _____

Nutritional Information Charts

GENERAL NUTRIENTS

Nutrient	Form	Sources
carbohydrates	sugar	honey, fruits, molasses, candy, cookies
	starch	bread, potatoes, rice, noodles, pastries
fats	vegetable fat	corn oil, olive oil, margarine
	animal fat	bacon grease, lard, butter
protein	meat	pork, beef, chicken, fish
	other	eggs, beans, peas, dairy products

MINERALS AND VITAMINS

Mineral/Vitamin	Sources
phosphorus	whole grains, meat, beans, peas
calcium	milk products, soybeans, tofu
iron	green leafy vegetables, peanuts, liver, dried fruit
vitamin A	all milk products, carrots
vitamin B^1	seafood, meat, whole grain, milk
vitamin B^2	eggs, fish, cheese, meat
vitamin B^6	whole grain, fish, meat
vitamin B^{12}	green vegetables
vitamin C	citrus fruits, tomatoes
vitamin D	fish, eggs, modern fortified milk

RECOMMENDED DAILY NUTRITION

Foods are organized into four groups. Each group has a recommended number of servings. Use the following chart of food groups and recommended servings to help you in analyzing the nutrition of a colonist and yourself.

bread/cereal group	noodles, bread, cereals	4/day
meat group	eggs, meat, fish, nuts	2/day
fruit/vegetable group	green and yellow vegetables and all fruits	4/day
dairy group	cheeses, yogurt, milk	4/day

CHAPTER THREE
Family Life

Family Membership

Who comprised the average colonial family? One belief that dominated early thinking was that the colonial family was an extended family comprised of parents or stepparents, many children, grandparents, servants, and others that may have been taken in out of charity such as widowed aunts, orphaned children, or unmarried spinsters. Given the harsh conditions of the early colonists, this seems to be a sound conclusion. Other facts, however, paint quite a different picture of the colonial family.

To understand how nearly impossible such an extended family was in the colonies, one only needs to look no further than the size of the house. The 20' x 20' floor plan with one and one-half stories that dominated many early New England houses would make it impossible for an extended family of more than five or six to live without great discomfort. Even the addition of a lean-to room that formed the typical salt-box style house did not make room for more than two more. These numbers hold up well when census information is examined. An average household in colonial New England contained two parents, three children, and on occasion a grandparent or servant/apprentice. Outside of New England this profile changes. In the South, for example, the unusually high mortality rate among women (especially in childbirth) and men (diseases) left a larger number of orphans and very few grandparents. Consequently, the profile of this typical family changes dramatically.

As might be expected a family went through a cycle. Two people recently married would have one child within the first year creating a household of three. That number would increase gradually with children being born about every two years. Census information verifies that this married couple would have many children in a lifetime, numbers as high as 26 are on record (Benjamin Franklin was one of 17), but the actual number of children living in one household was usually no more than three or four. Infant mortality reduced the number. Some were apprenticed to other households as early as 10 years old. Marriage resulted in almost immediate removal from the family home as well. Even with an occasional grandparent and servant or apprentice, the number in a family rarely went above six or seven. By the time the married couple reached middle age, they may very well have had no more than three in the house again.

Family Webs

In England the town or village was the center of most people's lives. The village took the responsibility of taking care of the destitute or decrepit or orphaned. In America this tradition did not hold. People lived in greater isolation in America due to the fact that they lived on farms and came into the village only for supplies, meetings, or entertainment. The sense of community that was so prevalent in England, however, did not disappear in America. It was instead transferred into another form, the family web.

People moving to America established farms situated away from but within traveling distance of a town. As the family grew older, children might move out of the household but would usually set up their respective homes on land near their parents. In fact, land and a house were part of a typical marriage arrangement between two families. After a few generations, a neighborhood of farms developed all made up of people of common kin. This neighborhood clan became what the English village was, an interconnected community system.

In the South where disease claimed so many more lives, this family web was most important in providing a support system. Outside the South, in the Middle Colonies as well as New England, this same pattern held. Despite the fact that marriages resulted in changing religious and ethnic backgrounds, the web of the family was tight, and the home became a gathering place for the many kinfolk during celebrations as well as funerals.

A profile of the American family household has changed over the years. A typical colonist's household in the 1690s contained an average of six people including two parents, three children, and either one grandparent or a servant/apprentice. The typical family structure of the colonial period has changed. People are having fewer children. Grandparents unable to take care of themselves may reside in nursing homes. Orphans are taken care of by state agencies, and few people have servants let alone apprentices living in their homes.

Purpose:

To accumulate data relevant to their own family and combine it with other classmates' data to create a profile of the typical family household.

Procedure:

1. On paper have students list the names of everyone living in their household and classify them as *parent, child, grandparent, aunt, uncle,* or *other* (identify the *other*).
2. Have students total each classification and also arrive at a grand total for the household.
3. You may want to further classify stepparents and stepchildren. This will create a more focused profile.
4. As a class, combine the data by developing totals for each classification (i.e., total parents, total children, total grandparents).
5. Divide the totals by the number of students in the class to arrive at a profile for the average household in your class.
6. Display the information on a bulletin board as illustrated below.

ACTIVITY   *Family Webs and Community Support*

In colonial America hard times were weathered by families sticking together. If an older family member became ill or indigent, it was the family that took care of things. If the head of a household became disabled, others in the clan took over the running of the farm. If money or land or property was needed, people turned to their kinfolk.

Today we have a much different system for handling special situations. Nursing homes are available for the elderly in need of care. Banks and lending institutions can lend money for special needs. Most noticeably, the government has a wealth of programs to assist people in need.

Purpose:

To discover what forms of community support exist today and contrast that support with what was available for the colonist. It will allow students to explore the use of nonconventional research sources and evaluate whether today's community/government support system is better or worse than the family web support of the colonist.

Procedure:

1. Arrange students into cooperative work groups.
2. Hand out the activity sheet entitled "Family Webs and Community Support." Discuss the introductory information related to how colonists relied on their families in dealing with the specific situations.
3. Have students brainstorm how those same five situations could be handled today and have them record their ideas.
4. Have students discuss these at home for additional ideas and share them in their groups.
5. Allow students to divide the situations among themselves and explore further the public and private support systems by contacting offices to find out who is eligible for the support, what benefits the office provides, who pays for it, and how.
6. Feel free to add or substitute more relevant situations on the activity sheet. For example, if your students are from a rural community, a situation might be "What if an important piece of farm equipment broke down just before harvest?"

Evaluation:

When students are done gathering information, have them prepare and present a group report that reflects all the information they accumulated. Then, in those same groups or as a class, discuss whether our system of public/private support is better for people than the colonists' system of family support. Key ideas might include quality of care versus expenses and personal concern versus bureaucratic handling.

Name _____

Family Webs and Community Support

Introduction:

Most colonists worked to remain independent. At times, however, situations arose that made people depend on others. In colonial America that support came from a person's larger family.

If an older family member was unable to care for himself or herself, one of the other family households took in the person. If the head of a household became disabled, others in the clan took over the running of the farm. If someone became ill, family members made visits to the home and cared for the ill person until the illness passed. If a child were orphaned, he or she was adopted by one of the other family members.

Today, similar situations arise that require people to seek help, but we no longer rely only on our larger family.

Directions:

Below is a list of four situations that require people to get help from someone. You are to first discuss these situations with your group members and list sources of help for each situation. Then you are to discuss these situations at home to obtain more information to share with the group.

1. Elderly Care
   If an older person in your family were unable to take care of himself or herself, what public and private agencies could help?

2. Unemployment
   If the wage earner(s) in your family suddenly became unemployed, how could your family get what it needs to live?

3. Child Care
   If your parent(s) needed to have a child watched eight hours a day, five days a week so that they could work, what could they do?

4. Disability
   If one of your parents became so ill that they needed daily care, how could that care be provided?

Follow-up:

Our society has developed many agencies to help people in situations just such as those listed above. Contact some of the agencies you listed as a group and find out who is eligible for the support, what benefits the office provides, who pays for it, and how.

CHAPTER FOUR

Women in Colonial America

Women in Jamestown

Today's method by which a young woman and a young man select each other for marriage is quite different from what the first colonists experienced. For the early colonists, marriages were often matters of legal convenience. Jamestown, which in its first years was perpetually on the verge of collapse, consisted almost wholly of men who had little stake in the New World. The House of Burgesses in Virginia issued a statement in 1619 granting 50 acres of land to every married woman coming to America. In 1620 the Virginia Company supplied 90 women to the colony. Upon arrival these women were promptly *auctioned off* for no less than 120 pounds of tobacco. This effort was so successful that in 1621 another 38 were auctioned off for 150 pounds of tobacco each. The record shows that this effort succeeded in turning around the work habits of the men. Before marriage they had little reason to work hard. With a wife and child, however, they worked hard to raise tobacco and make the money necessary to form a substantial household. Thus it was that some of the first marriages in America were more a matter of practicality than a matter of heart.

The legal aspect of courtship and marriage continued beyond these first years. Marriage held serious social and financial consequences to the early colonist and therefore became an arranged affair. Frequently, it was not the man and woman involved that did the arranging; it was their parents.

Courtship and Marriage

By custom, and in some colonies by law, suitors were expected to seek permission from the parents of the young lady to court her formally. Court records actually illustrate instances where young men were brought before a judge for attempting to win the favor of a young lady without first asking permission.

The woman, however, did have final say in many circumstances depending to a degree on the attitude of the head of the household as well as her own forcefulness in the matter. In families with a dominant father he became the sole arranger of the marriage to construct a family of wealth and proper social ties. In many recorded cases the father's wishes prompted his daughter to elope with the man of her choice, thereby sacrificing any property the lady might have brought into the marriage. In other families the father expected to give his approval only as a matter of custom leaving the real decision to the daughter.

A woman who was widowed showed quite a bit more independence in her selection and marriage to a man. Because she inherited much of the estate upon her husband's death, a widow commanded much more attention from suitors. She was not bound to anyone for permission and consequently was much more selective. In fact, the records show that many a widow initiated courtship with a widower because she foresaw the profit of the marriage.

Although today we see the prenuptial agreement as a modern contrivance, the same type of agreement was common in colonial days. The matter of property was usually negotiated between the families of the couple to marry. The parents of the suitor were expected to show that their son could provide for the lady and were expected to provide land and/or a house along with sufficient means to get started. In turn, the parents of the lady put up a dowry. Marriages did not take place when such financial arrangements could not be made.

If one or both of the couple had been previously married, the prenuptial agreement could be more extensive and demanding. Often an agreement had to be made as to whose property going into the marriage would remain whose. If children were involved, a widow might specifically state that upon death all property she brought into the marriage would first be divided among her offspring. Some agreements, however, went well beyond such legal matters. One woman would not agree to marriage until the man first promised to buy and keep a coach and second to wear a wig always. That marriage never took place.

This information about prenuptial agreements creates a picture of the colonial woman contrary to the popular image. Colonial women were independent and willful, and the laws supported such traits.

Throughout the colonies the actual courtship was more a matter of visitation than anything else. A suitor called upon the lady he intended to marry and they sat and talked. Sometimes gifts were exchanged. An effort was made to leave the young couple alone although among the poorer colonial families this was not easy in a one-room home. In the winter when being left alone in a cold, unheated room hardly lent itself to courtship, the practice of bundling was employed. The idea was to allow a woman and her suitor to get into bed wrapped tightly and separately to stay warm while still carrying on conversation. By the French and Indian War this custom was all but eliminated due to its lack of acceptance by the many immigrants coming to America.

After a suitable engagement period and after the dowry contract had been arranged, publishing of the banns (engagement announcement) occurred. In England such an announcement served to inform everyone in the village of the impending marriage in case of serious objection. In America, however, with farms so spread out, a new custom was devised. It was the marriage license. By issuing a license to all seeking marriage, the county clerk was able to keep track of marriages and thus prevent any improper ones.

Today, marriages are both civil and religious. In colonial New England they were purely civil. The magistrate performed the wedding. The Puritans did not want to mix ceremony with religion and did not allow the clergy to take part in it. After the wedding little was done in the way of revelry. Perhaps some refreshments were served, but that was all. By the end of the Colonial Era, however, weddings had become gala affairs in New England.

Marriage differed from area to area. In Pennsylvania the Quakers considered a couple married when they made a mutual pledge in the presence of the congregation during a meeting. No festivities followed. Among some of the Dutch, a man and a woman were permitted to live together after the banns were published. Little in the way of ceremony followed. Only in the South did festivity dominate the ceremony. Since the people of the South followed the Anglican church, the wedding was performed by the clergy. Guests then returned to the home where they celebrated long into the night. This is the tradition that spread. By the time of the American Revolution, wedding ceremonies and merrymaking were synonymous in all the colonies.

ACTIVITY *Wedding Ceremonies*

America is a nation of immigrants, all bringing with them their own culture and ceremonies. Although the early colonists had to abandon their own village wedding customs because village life simply did not develop in America, new customs eventually replaced them. As immigrants from other countries came to America and settled in close-knit groups, they retained many of the wedding ceremonies of their homelands and altered others to suit the situation. Today an abundance of wedding ceremonies exists in America reflecting religious beliefs as well as ethnic culture.

Purpose:

To become aware of the variety of wedding customs that exists in America and some of the meaning attached to these customs. Second, the activity encourages students to reflect on what elements are important in a wedding ceremony.

Procedure:

1. First decide how you want to work: individually, in pairs, or in small groups. If you have a culturally diverse class, pairs is most efficient. If your class (and community) is culturally homogenous, larger groups may be necessary so that students will find a variety of customs.

2. In completing part one of the activity sheet, "Weddings–Ceremonies With Meaning," the space provided can be used for a working draft. It would be best to have students prepare a final version on their own paper. Students can get information by first examining their own family's traditions. If that is fruitless, have them interview other teachers, or neighbors. Emphasize the need not only to learn what the custom is but also to learn the meaning behind the custom.

3. As a class share the different customs. Chart some of the information on the board.

4. In inventing their own wedding ceremony, again emphasize the need to have meaning behind each custom. As a class come up with a list of things students should consider in their design such as the following:

   a. traditions to be followed before the wedding.
   b. whether it will be a religious or civil ceremony.
   c. special vows or words spoken.
   d. specific actions to be performed during the ceremony.
   e. whether or not to include any festivity afterward.

5. Allow students to share and defend their designs.

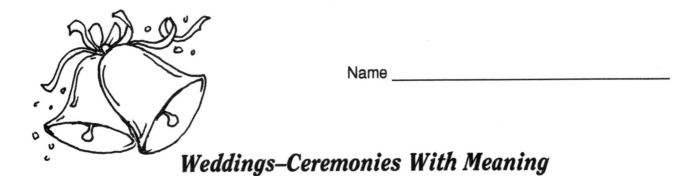

Name _____

Weddings–Ceremonies With Meaning

Part One: Investigating a Wedding Ceremony

You are to investigate the elements of a wedding ceremony. This can be a wedding ceremony that is part of your own family's customs or one that is part of another culture. On the lines below list meaningful elements of the ceremony and include an explanation of the meaning for the traditional parts of the ceremony. In your investigation pay attention to specific words that must be spoken during the vows, specific actions that must be performed by members of the wedding, and specific customs that are observed both before the wedding ceremony and during the festivities that follow.

_____

_____

_____

_____

_____

_____

_____

_____

Part Two: Developing Your Own Ceremony

As you can see, ceremonies and customs all have meaning behind them. The colonists that came from England had to abandon their village customs because in America they lived on isolated farms. After several generations village life began to reform in America, and wedding customs and traditions began anew.

If you were to develop your own wedding customs as some colonists did, what would you include? On your own paper invent your own wedding ceremony. Each decision you make should have some meaning behind it. Be ready not only to explain but also to defend all aspects of the ceremony to the class.

The New World . . . of Work

Wanted: a woman of singular beauty and virtue and unspoiled reputation to attend a home; must be industrious and pleasant, and able to run a household including cooking, cleaning, churning, combing, carding, spinning, knitting, pickling, candle making, as well as take part in the running of a farm as from time to time is necessary by milking, bee keeping, harvesting, threshing, and raising small livestock; must be willing to educate one young lady in the practice of economy, who with her father will compose a family.

The above want ad may seem ridiculous but was not so rare in colonial times. Widowers living in more isolated areas and seeking a wife published such ads. When looking at the list of duties, one has to wonder who would want such a position. In colonial New England, however, such a list of duties as above was considered normal for the woman of a household and, in fact, did not mention many other daily and seasonal chores.

The first generation of women in colonial America came to America under many different circumstances, but all ended up working hard to survive. As previously mentioned the first women in Jamestown were literally brought and auctioned to eligible bachelors. In all likelihood these women, like so many that followed, were indentured servants who may have been bankrupt or who were seeking new lives and better opportunities than those offered in England. Without the money necessary to travel to America, many became indentured to the captain or some other benefactor who then sold their indentures when they arrived in the New World.

This woman was approximately 17 to 23 years old. She not only wanted opportunities she would never be afforded in England, but she also wanted a husband. Being indentured, however, precluded her marrying until her four or five years of service had expired. America, however, was an especially trying place for those first-generation women. Malaria was not uncommon and often left women weak. The work was much harder than these women probably expected and there was no one to regulate the abuse that they might endure at the hands of the man or husband and wife that held the contract to the indenture. Some women never outlived their indenture. Those who did, married quickly.

Daily Life of the Colonial Woman

The early colonial households were almost 100 percent self-sufficient. Except for some sugar or linen goods which arrived occasionally by ship, everything a family had was produced in the home, and more likely than not it was produced by the woman. Life for the colonial woman was an unending string of chores—none of which could be ignored. If a woman was lucky enough to have several older children, they helped with these chores. Still, the main responsibility for getting everything done was hers.

Heat and Light

Central to the household was the fireplace. Everything depended on it, and it is not surprising that many chores involved its use. Therefore, keeping the fire going was of prime importance. Starting a fire from flint and steel was extremely tricky, taking a half an hour or more. Consequently, it was much better to make sure the fire never went out. At night the coals were banked and in the morning blown into a flame. Gathering wood, splitting it, and stacking it all became a woman's job although splitting the larger pieces was usually done by the husband. Cleaning the fireplace was a daily chore since ashes accumulated quickly in a fire that burned constantly.

A colonist relied on a variety of candles all of which needed attention. Rushlights were made by soaking the pith of a dried rush in grease. This was then held by the jaws of a special holder. The making of the rushlight and the constant tending of the light as it burned down was a chore. Candles eventually replaced these crude lamps, but it took a lot of time to make them. Tallow, a fat extract from sheep and cattle, was melted in a kettle and wicks tied to a pole were dipped, cooled, and dipped again repeatedly until a candle of sufficient thickness formed. This job was seasonal, usually being performed in the autumn when animals were slaughtered. It was an all-day job for several days because enough candles needed to be made to last a year. On a good day a woman could make a couple hundred candles.

Cooking

Cooking was a never-ending job. Everything the family ate had to be made from scratch. Corn had to be milled either with a samp mortar or with a small mill called a *quern*. The resultant corn-meal was used in the making of porridges, puddings, and breads. These meals, along with stews, made up the main fare on a daily basis. They required less tending than the more elaborate fried or broiled meats which required constant turning and tending to prevent burning. While a kettle of stew simmered, a woman was free to do other cooking-related tasks such as milking the cow, churning the butter, tending the garden in the summer, helping to slaughter animals in the autumn, as well as salting or smoking the meat.

Clothing

No one living in the colonies had the wardrobe found in today's homes. The average wardrobe consisted of two sets of clothing per person. All clothing was made in the home and involved many separate jobs.

If wool were used, it had to be first washed and dried and usually dyed at this time. Dying, of course, required the gathering and preparing of specific plants which was another chore. The washing and dying took out many natural oils so the dried wool needed to be saturated with oil or lard before being carded. Carding fluffed the wool making it possible to spin it (i.e., twist it into thread). Not every household had a spinning wheel, so in many cases a hand spindle had to do. The thread that was produced was woven on a loom into cloth about 30 inches wide. Three yards of cloth 30 inches wide was a good day's weaving. Finally with cloth available, the clothes could be hand sewn to fit any member of the household; blankets were also made in this fashion.

Flax was used to make linen and involved a 20-step process. These steps were so heavy handed and time consuming that they were often left for winter work when both the husband and wife could be involved. Flax was not commercially grown in New England until 1640 and wool production began after that. Consequently, people wore their clothes until they were literally worn out. It is no wonder that some of the first trades that developed in the colonies involved the making of clothing.

Cleaning

Besides cleaning the fireplace, general sweeping was as constant a job as cooking. Muddy boots and shoes tracked in plenty of dirt, requiring the floor to be swept several times daily. Cookware was also cleaned regularly (though not nearly as regularly as today's pots and pans cleaned in the sink or dishwasher). To do this task required water which, of course, had to be hauled in from outside. Therefore, early colonists built their homes near streams or lakes. Later, wells were dug. Either way the only method of getting the water was by a bucket at a time.

Bathing was infrequent by today's standards. Water in a bowl splashed upon the face and hands was the norm. Soap was used but had to be made in the home—once again by the woman. Ashes from the fire were layered in a barrel with straw. Water poured over this leached out lye. The lye was then combined with grease in a kettle and cooked (most definitely in the open air because of the unbelievably horrible odor) and stirred constantly. As it boiled down, a soft soap formed. If hard soap were needed, salt was added. This soap could then be used for the cleaning of clothing, although, again, this was much more infrequent than today.

Where Were the Men?

Considering all the work being done by women, one might conclude that the men were lazy sluggards living off the toil of their wives. This is a tempting conclusion but not valid. The success of living off the land depended upon getting crops planted. The rocky and unyielding soil of New England combined with the very poor farm tools available made planting and growing crops backbreaking work. Fields had to be cleared of trees using axes not designed for such work. Stumps had to be dug out and removed. The soil had to be prepared using a wooden plow that could barely turn over the soil without breaking. In addition planting, harvesting, threshing, mending tools, keeping the house weather tight and digging wells filled up the typical man's day.

The division of labor we often associate with men and women today may very well not have existed in colonial America especially in the seventeenth century. Numerous researchers refer to the relationship between husband and wife as a partnership. Both wanted to succeed and shared the labor (enough of which to keep 10 people busy). In the end, a woman in colonial America could be found helping with harvest as easily as a man could be found making soap.

Required Other Duties

The chores of the keeping of a household did not stop here. Whatever arose that needed to be done became part of daily life. Infants and very young children needed to be tended and watched. Later their education became the woman's duty. If a household kept bees, which many did, beekeeping was added to the list. When things broke or tore, mending was necessary.

Not only were there a large number of jobs, but most jobs were quite difficult. In fact, very few jobs involved just one step. Arriving at a finished product such as clothing, soap, or a meal involved many tasks. The women colonists of New England during the seventeenth century took on all or most of these chores. Indentured servants helped relieve the woman of some of this work but only if she were wealthy enough to purchase one. In the South, where plantations were staffed by slaves, women were involved less with daily chores but were more responsible for overseeing the work. Plantations were much larger and their operations much more involved. Consequently, a woman living on a southern plantation still had a full day's work.

Into the eighteenth century, village life began to change the amount and type of work for women. Men who had worked a farm now practiced a trade or a business in the village. Consequently, bartering and purchasing made it possible to obtain items that earlier were only made in the home. Women became involved in the businesses; and if their husbands died, they may even have run them.

ACTIVITY   *Want Ads*

Have students develop a set of want ads. After being exposed to the life of a colonial woman, have them develop a want ad that a widower might design. It should not be deceptive but should include at least a partial list of duties, skills, expectations, and living conditions.

Following this want ad, have students write similar ones based on the role of today's woman. Use the same basic guidelines but beforehand have students discuss in small groups what kinds of skills, expectations, and duties women of today must confront.

Students may also enjoy developing a third want ad, one advertising for the position of a teacher. They will have a lot of fun with this assignment regardless of the fact that today's teachers are not necessarily women.

WANTED:
☞ A FEW GOOD WOMEN ☜

The Role of a Woman in Colonial America

Many women came to America to find a better life. They were indentured servants (in some cases auctioned off for tobacco), who faced many hardships. These hardships included not only the unending work described in this chapter but many others as well.

The first leading cause of death was childbirth. There were no doctors or hospitals. Children were born with the help of a midwife, if they were lucky. The cold and unstable environment of New England and the high incidence of disease in the South were hazards for both the mother and child. Men generally outlived women in colonial times. Women, however, who made it past their childbearing years usually outlived their husbands. Nonetheless, the high death rate of infants only added to the grief of a colonial woman's life.

Since the colonial woman worked so closely with the fire, she often risked dangerous burns. It was not uncommon for these burns to create infections that led to death. In fact, the second leading cause of death for the colonial woman was infection caused by burns.

The life of a colonial woman was a paradox. In the early colonial days men and women were more partners in the effort to succeed on the farm. Laws were developed that specifically called for the sharing of property equally and for the caring of widows should the husband die. As time progressed and the move was made to towns and cities, the role of women in the household changed as did their status. Legally, they became inferior to men. By law they could not vote or hold office. In some colonies they could not own a business. Marriage was expected of all young women, and staying unmarried was a social scandal. Religion, which dominated some communities like that of the Puritans, further promoted the inferiority image. It was the women, after all, who were always accused of witchcraft–never the men. In reality, however, women were strong, inventive, and courageous in the early colonial times; and they were often the brains, innovation, and drive behind a successful businessman in later years.

ACTIVITY   *A Diary*

Many a person kept a diary in colonial times. In fact, much of what we know about the Colonial Era comes from three sources: public records, letters, and diaries or journals.

Have students create diary entries for a colonial woman. Have them focus on not only what she had to go through but also what she must have thought and felt. Have students select specific situations to write about (e.g., the death of a child, arriving as an indentured servant, waiting to see whether her parents will approve a marriage). Students can share these diary entries in groups or with the entire class.

An important follow-up discussion can focus on how the role of women has changed in 350 years in America. Students can discuss how the role has changed and whether they think the change is good. Finally, they can discuss how the role of women continues to evolve.

Cooking on an open fireplace was quite a bit different from cooking with electricity or gas. Cooking times varied, and the heat of the fire was not constant. The cooking utensils also had to be different. Most utensils were long handled or designed to be lifted from the fire with a long pole. Some were made of metal but others were made of wood. Very few could be found in their original form in today's kitchen.

The activity sheet entitled "What in the World Is This?" will give students an opportunity to match pictures of utensils used by colonial women with their descriptions and in some cases, their names. A similar activity that deals with tools can be found in Chapter One.

The utensils pictured were common, but it must be remembered that in any colonial household a husband or wife might design a special tool to suit his or her needs. This inventiveness sometimes gave rise to a new utensil that everyone in the colony soon wanted.

Below is the answer key to the activity. You will need to run off both the clue page and the utensil drawing page.

Answers to "What in the World Is This?"

1.	b	bread toaster		7.	c	trencher
2.	f	fire scoop		8.	h	trammel
3.	i	sugar cutter		9.	d	gridiron
4.	a	quern		10.	k	butter churn
5.	e	spider		11.	g	waffle iron
6.	l	samp mortar		12.	j	bellows

What in the World Is This?

Directions: Match the description found on this page to the pictures of cooking and eating utensils on the next page by writing the name of the utensils on the blank beneath the picture. There are no repeated sets and all descriptions and pictures are used.

a. This utensil was used to grind corn into corn meal. A larger version was attached to a windmill. It was called a *quern*.

b. This utensil was used to toast bread. If you look closely, you will see that it may even have left a pattern on the toast. It was simply called a *bread toaster*.

c. Colonists used this utensil to eat the many stews and porridges that made up their daily diet. It was called a *trencher*.

d. When colonists wanted to broil meat and save the drippings, they used this utensil. It was called a *gridiron*.

e. This cooking utensil allowed colonists to fry items in the fireplace without having to stand and hold the pan. It was called a *spider*.

f. If the fire went out, a person was sent to another house to get some hot coals to start a new fire. This *fire scoop* was used to transport the hot coals.

g. Today we can buy frozen waffles, but making a waffle over the fire required this *waffle iron*.

h. A *trammel* was used to adjust the height of hanging kettles over a fire.

i. Sugar, when it could be bought, was sold in large solid cones. To get a piece you would need this *sugar cutter*.

j. Getting the fire going required lots of air. Just blowing on it could make a person dizzy. This utensil blew air on the fire. It was called a *bellows*.

k. For colonists the old fashioned way to grind corn was to use the *samp mortar*. The corn was literally pounded into meal.

l. Turning cream into butter required backbreaking, muscle aching work at this *butter churn*.

Name _____

Directions: Below the picture of each colonial cooking utensil, write its name.

1. _____	7. _____
2. _____	8. _____
3. _____	9. _____
4. _____	10. _____
5. _____	11. _____
6. _____	12. _____

Since many utensils were invented and designed to fit colonial open hearth cooking, they can no longer be found in today's kitchen. Today's cooking utensils, however, are no less confusing if one has never seen them. Tea infusers, orange peelers, cheese or egg cutters, and miniature funnels are just a few examples of today's cooking utensils that some students would find strange.

You can recreate the identification exercise by bringing or having students bring utensils used around the house that others may not be able to identify easily. Create a display as part of a learning center and have students spend a couple class periods trying to identify their uses.

As a variation have students bring in obsolete cooking utensils that date back 10 to 50 years that their parents may still have. This gives them the opportunity to see the evolution of some of these utensils.

ACTIVITY   *Invent Your Own*

For their own convenience, comfort, or necessity, colonists were constantly designing or modifying utensils in the home. A warming pan (pictured) had hot coals placed in it and was then passed between the sheets to warm the bed before the colonist retired for the night. A foot stove (also pictured) was used in a similar way except that one's feet were placed on it, and heat radiating from the holes kept them warm.

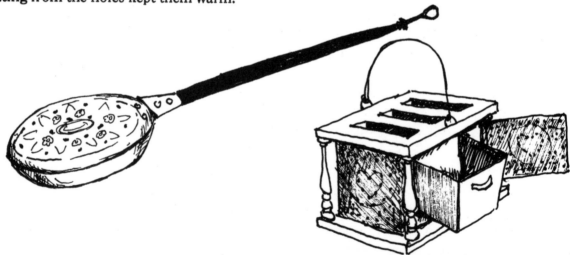

Just as the colonists did, students have needs for special tools or utensils. Height or lack of adult strength sometimes prevents adolescents from doing things or using things adults take for granted. Challenge students to design their own utensil or tool for a problem in their lives.

To do this students must first decide on a small problem they or someone in their family has. This can only be done through observation. They may notice a younger brother or sister struggling to reach something. They may observe a grandparent unable to open something.

Students can do this activity individually or in pairs. They first identify a real problem in their lives or someone else's life. They then work to design on paper an inventive solution. Finally, if possible, they make the invention. You can create a display of such inventions as students finish them.

Below are several writing activities designed to get students to work with some of the ideas discussed in this chapter. None are intended to be well-developed, report-style writings. Students should have fun working with these individually, in pairs, or in small groups.

1.   The Marriage License

What information is on a marriage license today? Have a few students investigate what information is required when applying for today's license. Have students speculate what information would have been needed on a marriage license in colonial times.

Finally, have students design their own marriage licenses that reflect what they think is important. The license can be further made into a document with some sort of border or illustrations.

2.   A Toast!

As wedding celebrations evolved in the colonies, one tradition developed that is still observed today. It is the act of toasting the bride and groom. A typical toast honors the bride and groom with compliments to their virtues and then wishes them good fortune in some specific way.

Have students write a toast for a colonial couple. What virtues might the toastmaker extol regarding the groom? The bride? What might the toastmaker wish for this couple? (Many children? Good health? Fields growing thick with corn?)

Now, have students prepare a toast for a modern couple. The virtues of a modern couple might be different as certainly would the wishes for them. These toasts can be presented in class orally with small cups of apple juice or water as each toast is raised.

3.   The Dowry

Both the bride and groom were expected in colonial times to bring property into a marriage. The groom usually had the lion's share to bring. A house, land, or some means of support were expected. The bride's dowry included her trousseau but also might include livestock, kitchen utensils, or even money.

Have students list what they own right now in their lives that they could take into a marriage. Share these lists in class. (Toys, games, bikes, and clothes will most likely lead lists.)

What kind of a dowry would be suitable for today's woman? In pairs or small groups, have students discuss this question and create a list of likely items for a modern dowry. Tell students to be prepared to present and defend their choices to the class.

CHAPTER FIVE

Life as a Colonial Child

Dangers and Diseases

If life was hard for adults in the early colonies, it was equally hard for children. Early life was the most dangerous of times. Infant mortality by today's standards was very high. Infant mortality was 10 percent, but that number reflects only those children dying within the first months of life. The number increases to 25 percent if we examine how many children actually reached maturity. Compared to today's low infant mortality of about 1 percent, these numbers seem astronomical. These numbers, however, are relative. A child born in England at the same time had an even smaller chance of surviving the first year because of the poorer nutrition available there. Women died in childbirth twice as often as children (one in five).

What accounted for these deaths? In the South malaria was a debilitating disease that often weakened mothers to the point of endangering their lives as well as their babies' lives. Difficult births (e.g., breech births) were not handled in the routine way they are today. Children were born in the home under the care of the older women of the colony who acted as midwives and advisors. They relied on their experiences which were sometimes inadequate in handling an unusual situation. Once born, a variety of dangers awaited a child. The threat of disease persisted and was compounded by incorrect medical practices. (See Chapter 7.) Nutritional deficiencies weakened children and made them susceptible to illness. In some households the fear of infant death prevented the parents from naming their children for six months to see whether the baby would live.

Natural dangers of the environment also presented a problem. Chief among these were burns caused by children getting too close to the fire. There are recorded instances of children actually falling into the fire. This seems almost unimaginable, but a lack of supervision is understandable given the fact that women had so many more chores to complete in a day's time and men were rarely in the house during the day. By today's standards, children were left unattended a good deal of the time exposing them to indoor as well as outdoor dangers. Injuries to children who fell into creeks and lakes or were cut by sharp objects or were trampled by livestock made life dangerous.

ACTIVITY   *Safety Survey*

Compared to our colonial counterparts, we are tremendously safety conscious. Our schools have safety patrols, we teach railroad and traffic safety, and some cities have safety programs called Safety Town that most five year olds attend before entering school. Perhaps our world is no less dangerous than it was 350 years ago, but the types of dangers have changed.

Purpose:

To analyze the dangers present in our world today and contrast them with those that may have been present in colonial times. Students will also observe safety precautions initiated in their own homes.

Procedure:

1. Have students speculate on possible safety hazards that colonial children may have faced. As a class develop a list.
2. In small, working groups have students list the types of safety hazards they face in their environment today. It might be helpful to do this by considering the dangers children face at different times in their lives. For example, an infant might fall down the steps when first learning to walk but faces the danger of being hit by a car or even abducted when old enough to play alone.
3. Discuss these as a class and create a master list.
4. As a follow-up activity have students individually list safety precautions that have been a part of their lives at home in dealing with these hazards. Have them share these in their groups the next day.
5. Finally, have students develop a list of safety rules or actions they would have initiated for a colonial child.
6. Use student ideas to create a bulletin board of colonial safety. Divide the board into sections with each section containing a rule and an illustration.

What's in a Name?

The first thing parents give their child is a name. As time goes by, the name is frequently re-fashioned (Thomas becomes Tom, Roberta becomes Bobbi, Margaret becomes Peggy, and William Joseph becomes Billy Joe), but the original idea remains. The cultural diversity of the people of the United States has brought a wealth of given names to our country. Some of these include Micho (Serbian), Akeesha (African-American), Antonio (Italian), Constance (English), and Carlos (Hispanic). Compared to other countries, Americans are used to seeing and pronouncing names that are different from their own. But even by today's standards, the names that colonial parents gave their children are unusual.

The Puritans had a penchant for assigning their children Biblical names. Thus, names such as Moses, Gershom, Sarah, Hannah, Abijah, Joseph, and Samuel were not uncommon. Another common practice was to name children after desired character traits. From this we see colonial names such as Remember Allerton (a girl), Resolved White (a boy), Desire Minter (a girl), and Humility Cooper (a girl). All of these are the names of children who came over on the *Mayflower*. Other colonial given names include Patience, Charity, Faith, Love, Preserved, Unity, Supply, Restore, Hoped For, and Return. Circumstance also affected a child's name. After the death of her husband, one woman named her baby Father Gone.

| ACTIVITY | *Working With Names* |

Purpose:

To interpret some colonial names and devise names that reflect character traits.

Procedure:

1. Distribute copies of the activity sheet entitled "What's in a Name?" Working individually or in pairs, have students complete part one in which they speculate on why specific names were given to colonial children. Assign as many as you want the students to do.
2. Allow students to share their ideas in larger groups or as a class.
3. Have students work individually to devise names for their family members including themselves that reflect either a character trait or circumstance surrounding that person's birth. This is best done at home where parents can supply information.
4. Share these in class. Then develop and display a poster containing students' given names and invented names.

What's in a Name?

Some people love their names, and some people would love to change their names. Whatever the case most of us had no choice in the names we have. Where do these names originate? Sometimes we are named after others, relatives, or famous people. Sometimes names are chosen because parents think they sound good. In other instances names have special meanings.

Colonial names often fell into the latter category. Children received names that reflected a character trait the parents hoped he or she would develop. Thus, names like Patience, Charity, and Comfort were given. In other cases a child was named because of circumstances surrounding his or her birth. Fortune, Endurance, and Father Gone are examples of this.

Part One: Interpreting Names

Below is a list of real colonial names. Try to imagine why a child was given such a name by writing an explanation of the name as though you were the colonial parent giving the name. Do this on your own paper. Be ready to share your ideas in class.

Patience	Love	More Mercy	Silence
Temperance	Hoped For	Restore	Charity
Hope Still	Mercy	Deliverance	Submit
Thanks	Reform	Father Gone	Supply
Wait	Restore	Experience	Wait Still

Part Two: Giving Names

Now, imagine that you could rename all the members of your family in colonial fashion. That is, you could give them names that either reflect a character trait of theirs or a circumstance surrounding their births. Prepare a list of given names for your family members. You may want to consult with members of your family to find out whether any special event occurred around the time of another family member's birth. Remember that only names with a positive association were given. Be ready to share these in class and explain your decisions.

Daily Work of a Child

The amount of work on a farm during the early colonial days required that it be shared by everyone. For children this meant that they became part of the household work force at an early age. A child of three or four could rock a baby brother or sister. By the time a child was six or seven regular chores were part of his/her routine. The type of work depended only on how tall and strong the child had grown. Weeding the garden or flax fields, churning butter, or stirring a stew or porridge could be done by children relatively unsupervised. More intricate tasks such as spinning, milking, cooking, and candle making were taught to children as parents supervised the task. Older children were expected to supervise and instruct the younger ones.

The work world of children was a necessity brought about by harsh, pioneer-like conditions of early colonial living. As civilization progressed and populations shifted to the cities, the drudgery of so much daily work was lifted and replaced by education, games, and other pastimes.

Butter Churning

Young children of 9, 10, or 11 had the strength to do this simple but time-consuming task and were often given the job. After milking, the milk was allow to separate. The cream which rose to the top was skimmed and poured into the churn. Five or more gallons of the cream were churned at a time depending on the size of the churn. The churn looked like a wooden bucket that narrowed at the top and had a lid with a hole in the center. A paddle with a long stick attached called a *dasher* was then placed in the churn. The lid was replaced and the children began the arduous task of moving the dasher up and down.

The amount of time it took to turn the cream into butter varied with the temperature, type, and amount of milk and diligence of the child. Thirty to forty minutes was typical. To pass the time children would recite rhymes. First the cream got foamy. Then globs of butter fat would separate from the milk. The butter was cleaned from the dasher and removed from the churn. The remaining milk was called buttermilk and used for drinking.

On a wooden board the butter was cleaned with cold water and shaped into cakes by using two paddles. It was also common to draw or press a design on these cakes.

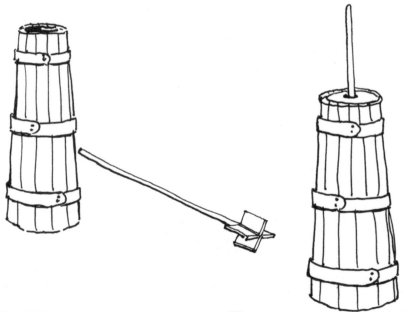

Churning Butter the Modern Way

This activity can be done easily and quickly in one class period. It allows all children to be involved and allows them to experience the way cream turns to butter. You may want to discuss that butter is really the animal fat found in milk. Churning separates the fat from the milk. The percent number assigned to milk we buy in the store is its butterfat content. Thus, two percent milk has two percent butterfat, whole milk has about three and one-half percent, and skim milk has zero percent.

Purpose:

To witness the changing of cream into butter.

Materials:

1. one or two clean, quart-sized glass jar(s) with screw-top lid(s)
2. mixing bowl
3. ice cubes or access to a refrigerator
4. butter knives
5. one or two pints of heavy cream or whipping cream
6. salt
7. plain white bread

Procedure:

1. Place the one pint of cream in the glass jar and secure it with the screw-top lid. Butter will form best if cool cream is used.
2. Allow students to take turns shaking the jar. For a large class you may want to have two going at once.
3. After 15 minutes or less, the butterfat will separate from the buttermilk in several globs. Pour off the buttermilk carefully. Students can taste the buttermilk.
4. Sprinkle lightly with salt. (Optional–most of the butter bought in a store is salted. Unsalted butter is called sweet butter.)
5. Cool the butter in a refrigerator or bowl with ice. This will make it workable.
6. Once it has stiffened, have one group of students divide and shape it into small cakes using butter knives. Then have another group fashion designs to put on each cake.
7. Serve with plain white bread to enhance the fresh taste of the butter.

Butter Churning Rhyme

To help pass the time during the monotony of churning butter, and to keep the churning going at a steady pace, children often recited rhymes. One very popular rhyme is repeated below. Any student's name can be substituted in line three as students churn their own butter in class.

Come butter come,
Come butter come.
Johnny standing at the gate,
Waiting for a butter cake.
Come butter come.

The rhyme has a definite beat to it with the accent occurring almost every other syllable.

Cóme bút-ter cóme

Jóhn-ny stánd-ing át the gáte

Have students invent their own five-line rhyming poem using the same beat pattern. They can begin easily by just replacing the third and fourth lines of the above rhyme and then get more inventive by designing an entirely new poem. The challenge is to have them keep the proper beat pattern that a person would use while churning butter.

Toys and Games

With all the work required of a colonial family, one would hardly think that there would be time for fun and games. To a degree that was true. If we look at the early colonists, the demand that work put on each family member's time certainly precluded much leisure activity. Some religious groups such as the Puritans also discouraged play time because they saw it as idleness and unnecessary. Cotton Mather, one of the more influential Puritan ministers, spoke against play as the first sign of a child's fall from grace. (Interestingly, one of his own sons, Samuel, loved to play which frustrated and vexed Cotton.) As the Colonial Era progressed, however, and the population moved to cities, the profile of the American child changed. More time was available for games and toys. By the middle of the eighteenth century well-to-do merchants could buy toys made by woodcrafters.

Despite lack of time and religious roadblocks, play for children was too natural to be completely obliterated. Toys and games surfaced. All of them were homemade varieties. Cornhusk dolls, games of tag, hoop rolling, hop scotch, huzzlecap, and stoolball were all games and toys that were invented using objects available around the farm. What could not be found might be whittled. Tops, whirligigs, apple dolls, and yo-yos fell into this category. Below is a short glossary of colonial childhood games and toys. You may want to pose these to students and have them guess what it was or how it was played.

whirligig	– a toy made in the shape of a little man with movable arms that whirled in the wind
huzzlecap	– also called chuck-farthing or pitch penny; a game in which pennies were pitched into a cap
stoolball	– a game similar to baseball or cricket; a ball is bowled at a three-legged stool defended by a batter
hoop roll	– a toy/game in which a hoop from a barrel is rolled using a stick
apple dolls	– a doll body whittled from wood that has a dried apple head
honey pot	– a game in which one child rolls up tight like a honey pot while the others try to lift and carry him/her
cratch cradle	– also called cat's cradle; one player weaves string between outstretched fingers and another player removes the string without dropping the loops to produce another woven figure; a *cratch* was a grated crib or manger

Tag is a game older than the colonists themselves. The activity sheet entitled "Tag . . . You're It" lists some of the different types of tag without any explanation of the rules. Your students can speculate how each was played and share their ideas. Hopefully, in the colonial spirit of invention, discussion will get students to design some of their own games of tag. In writing the rules to their own game of tag, students will experience the necessity of writing precise directions.

Tag . . . You're It

All games played by colonial children had to be invented and played with whatever was available around the farm. Scarce resources were seldom used for games and toys, so the likeliest games involved no parts except the player's own imagination in making up the rules.

Tag was a favorite because it could be played anywhere and needed nothing but two or more people. Colonial children made up their own rules for tag. Below are listed five types of tag played by colonial children. There is no record of the rules. After each one write a brief explanation of how you think it was played.

1. stone-tag _____
_____
_____

2. cross-tag _____
_____
_____

3. squat-tag _____
_____
_____

4. tell-tag _____
_____
_____

Invent Your Own

Invent your own form of tag. On your own paper explain the rules of play and give the game a name.

ACTIVITY   *Cornhusk Dolls*

Dolls have been a part of most children's worlds for centuries. In colonial times children's dolls were made from what was available, and at harvest time cornhusks were the most plentiful things around. Many colonial mothers saved cornhusks to make dolls for their daughters by the holidays.

The following explanation of how to make cornhusk dolls has been adapted from several sources. It is not totally authentic, but it is a method that works with children in small and even larger groups. It is best done all at once and will require over an hour if you have alert, cooperative students. If you need to break it up into two class periods, the activity can be done by doing steps one through six one day and the rest the next day. Gathering and preparing materials beforehand cuts down on class time needed for the project. It is also possible to work with a partner. The string tying while holding cornhusks in place may be frustrating for some students.

Materials:

cornhusks – Fresh, inner green husks is the least expensive way to go. Get students to bring these to class.

newspaper
scissors
large bowl or basin with warm water
kite string
pipe cleaner or lightweight wire for arms
white glue
felt–gray or brown for authenticity
felt tip marker

Procedure:

1. Dry the inner green husks on newspapers covered by another sheet of newspaper. Allow one or two days for them to turn yellow.
2. Soak the dried husks in warm water for about 10 minutes to make them pliable. Remember that when working with the husks, keep them moist and keep the smooth side of the husk turned out.
3. Layer five to seven husks together as though you were putting them around an invisible rod. Tightly tie them in the middle with string.
4. Pull down the husk above the knot as though you were peeling a banana.

5. Work the folded top part into a rounded head. Wrap and tie string about one inch from the top to form a head.

6. Roll another piece of cornhusk around the pipe cleaner and tie it in several places. Keep this thin.

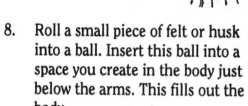

7. Insert the arm between the husks of the body just below the head.

8. Roll a small piece of felt or husk into a ball. Insert this ball into a space you create in the body just below the arms. This fills out the body.

9. To make the bodice, cut two pieces of felt into strips. Place them over the shoulders of the doll allowing them to criss-cross in the front and back. Tie them at the waist to secure them or glue them.

10. Make a skirt out of felt, and glue it at the waist.

11. Using the felt tip marker, draw a face on the doll.

12. Using cornhusks, felt, sticks, and other suitable materials, make accessories for the doll such as a broom, a purse, or a cap.

A diamanté poem is a style of poetry marked by certain characteristics. First, it deals with opposites or contrasting ideas as its subject. Second, its finished shape is that of a diamond. Third, each line has a specific type and number of words.

Lines one and seven name the opposites or contrasting ideas–one word each.
Lines two and six give adjectives describing each opposite–two words per line.
Lines three and five give three -ing verbs (participles) relating to each opposite–three words each.
Line four lists four nouns. The first two nouns relate to the first opposite and the second two nouns relate to the second opposite.

The following example uses the contrasting ideas of the sun and moon as the subject.

Sun
Hot, bright
Beginning, Searing, Illuminating
Morning,   Noon,   Evening,   Night
Ending, Quieting, Sleeping,
Subdued, Cool
Moon

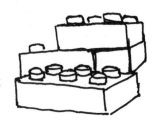

Purpose:

To contrast elements of a colonial child's life with those of a child's life today.

Procedure:

1. In small groups have students list many ways that a child's life in the colonies is different from a child's life today. Included should be elements such as daily life, work expectancy, and toys and games. Share these as a class.
2. Introduce the diamanté format. Provide the rules and an example. Perhaps develop one as a class.
3. Allow students to select some aspect of colonial life for children to contrast with the way it is today.

Note:

The first and seventh lines of the poem are supposed to be single word opposites or contrasting ideas. That can be a problem with this format. "Colonial Toys" . . . "Modern Toys" are two words apiece. To avoid this problem students can make the title of the poem the contrasting ideas, and the first and seventh lines then can be "Then" . . . "Now" or "Colonial" . . . "Modern."

ACTIVITY *A Colonial Child's Diary*

Purpose:

To allow students to become aware of their own everyday life style. To allow students to speculate on the daily lifestyle of a colonial child. To allow students to observe and evaluate the differences between these two daily life styles.

Procedure:

1. Over a three- to five-day period have each student keep a journal that focuses on the daily events of their lives. At first students will tend to record only what they did as in a log. Encourage students to reflect on these events and include some writing on their feelings regarding what happened during the day. You can encourage this by keeping your own journal/diary and sharing it with them.
2. During this same time span have each student keep a separate diary for a child living during the colonial time period. This will require that they consider what took up the child's time. Again, encourage them to be reflective and write about how the colonial child felt about this life style.
3. In groups or as a class, share these journal entries. Discuss which life style is more appealing. Which had more responsibilities? Which allowed more freedom? Which is preferred?

Alternative Diary Activity:

A book by Margaret Pumphrey entitled *Pilgrim Stories* chronicles the immigration of the Pilgrims on the *Mayflower* and the first year in America. The interesting twist to this story is that it focuses on the children. At the end of the book it lists the 27 children that came over on the *Mayflower* and survived that first year. It is an Apple Paperback, Scholastic Inc., ISBN 0-590-45202-9.

Another way to get students writing about daily colonial life as a child is to read them all or part of *Pilgrim Stories* one chapter at a time. Begin by assigning them the role of one of the 27 children. After each chapter reading, have them write a diary entry that reflects what they just learned in the chapter as the character they have been assigned.

As with the above exercise, they will at first simply record what they heard, writing in first person. Encourage them to write down how they feel about the events as they happen.

CHAPTER SIX
Colonial Education

Simple But Necessary

Education in colonial times was less of a lifelong process than it is today. Most education was viewed as vocational. In the home children were taught as soon as possible how to perform jobs that they would need to do as adults. Parents were the sole teachers. For the girls of the early colonial period this included soap making, candle making, and all domestic chores. Boys learned many of these tasks, but by the time they were 12 or 13 they began to learn the jobs involved in raising crops including threshing, harvesting, and planting.

Reading and writing might have been taught in the home if the parents knew how themselves. The Massachusetts Bay Colony was so concerned about education that in 1642 it passed a law requiring education for children to the extent that a child could be taken from his/her home and apprenticed if the parents were not seeing to his/her education. Like so many laws, however, it was not enforced with much regularity. To further encourage education, in 1647 Massachusetts passed a law requiring towns to establish schools based on the number of households. This was the advent of our free and public education today. Other New England colonies followed Massachusetts' lead.

Education in New England

Boys especially were expected to learn to read and write. This would enable them to take care of legal matters with which women need not concern themselves. In practice, however, a colonial parent wanted all his/her children to read and write if one of them could. In many New England villages, dame schools were established for this purpose. They were so named because they were run by a woman who charged a small fee to teach students their letters, reading, and writing.

Education in the Southern Colonies

In the southern colonies home education prevailed as well. The fact that the population was so scattered contributed to home education. The type of person immigrating to these colonies, however, was distinctly different from the northern colonial. Southern colonial landowners were of two classes: wealthy plantation owner and poor farmer. The wealthy landowner had many ties to England and viewed himself first and foremost as a citizen of England. Chances are he was educated in England and was sent to the colonies to oversee the production of tobacco for a company (or was born to a family fitting that description). Thus, he was well educated and promoted the same education in his children. It was not uncommon for wealthy plantation owners to hire private tutors (usually divinity students), and some later sent their children to England to finish their education.

The poor farmer was most likely an indentured servant who had worked out his time and had managed to buy a small plot of land. He might have learned his ABCs as a servant but received little more than that. Consequently, he had less of an education tradition to pass on to his children. These small farmers usually organized "old field schools." These were the equivalent of the New England dame school. The local clergyman was the schoolmaster and held classes between April and September (the off-season for tobacco growing).

ACTIVITY   *How Long Does It Take to Get an Education?*

The amount of time students today spend in our compulsory education system far outweighs the amount of time their colonial counterparts spent. The activity sheet entitled "A Lifetime of Education" allows students to use their math skills in closely estimating the amount of time they have spent in school so far. It also gets them to estimate the amount of time a colonial child would have spent in school for the purpose of comparison. Finally, it provides a format for extrapolating how much more time they will spend getting an education. This activity can be done individually or in pairs and with or without calculators.

Name _____

A Lifetime of Education

In the Colonies

In the southern colonies children attended "old field schools." Children went to school five months of the year, April through August. School was open five days per week. Children began attending when they were about 7 and quit when they were about 12. These numbers represent the maximum amounts for most children.

Use the formula below to calculate the amount of time a southern colonial child spent in school. Use a calendar to help add the number of days in April through August.

# of school days per year   x   # of years = total days in school

The school day was eight hours long. Multiply the total days in school by eight to find out the total hours this same child could have spent in school.

Today

You can figure out how long you have been going to school using the same formula. Your teacher can help you find out how many school days there are in your school year, and you can figure out the length of each school day in hours. The chart below will help you organize the data. If you went to kindergarten half days, divide that year's number by two.

Grade	Total Days	x	Hours/Day	=	Total Hours in School
K	_____		_____		_____
1	_____		_____		_____
2	_____		_____		_____
3	_____		_____		_____
4	_____		_____		_____
5	_____		_____		_____
6	_____		_____		_____
8	_____		_____		_____

If you went to preschool or summer school, calculate those hours and add them to your total. Now, figure the grand total. You can also use the same formula to figure out how much time you will spend in class by the time you graduate from high school.

Learning to Read

Even though reading and writing are taught together in schools today, this was not so in colonial schools. The Puritan tradition of education encouraged reading to help enlighten the soul by reading the Bible. The percentage of university-trained people in New England during this time was greater than today.

Of the three *Rs* only reading was promoted in Puritan colonies. After all, reading helped to promote salvation by "studying the word of God," but writing did not. Consequently, the number of people who had the ability to write and do math was contrastingly low when compared to the number of readers. Outside Puritan New England, the other two *Rs* were give better attention.

The Hornbook

The first step in learning to read was to learn the alphabet. This was usually done with a book that was not really a book at all. It was called a hornbook. It was made of a thin piece of flat wood often with a handle fashioned at the bottom. Attached to it was a piece of paper on which was written the alphabet and below that simple syllables such as *ab, as, at, ib, el,* and *or*. This was followed by the Lord's Prayer. The paper was covered with a thin, transparent sheet made from the horn of a bull or other animal, thus helping to preserve it.

The Primer

The next tool in the reading process was the primer. Most famous among these was the *New England Primer*. For over 100 years this was the book that students throughout the colonies used to practice their reading. Over three million were printed, and the *New England Primer* eventually became the first book of millions of children.

It contained an alphabet, a table of syllables called a syllabrium, prayers, a list of men's and women's names, a short catechism of questions and answers related to God and religion, and in later editions short stories. Most notable in the *New England Primer,* however, were the sets of rhymes used to help students practice their reading. Each letter of the alphabet had a rhyme in which a key word that began with that letter appeared. An illustration accompanied each one.

A –   In *Adam's* Fall
We Sinned All.

H –   My Book and *Heart*
Shall never part.

N –   *Nightingales* sing
In Time of Spring.

Two-thirds of the rhymes were religious in nature. It is also interesting to note that today's rules of capitalization were obviously ignored.

Writing

When writing was taught, it was done with much more difficulty than can be imagined today. First of all, writing material was in short supply. Paper was rare. Households often kept scraps in safe, dry places. Schools were not privy to such a precious commodity. Consequently, another type of writing material was found, birch bark. Although clumsy and delicate, there was plenty of it available. Later, in better equipped schools, slates with chalk could be used to practice writing. Writing utensils were also rare by today's standards. A plummet or small ball of lead was a child's first writing tool. It was made of genuine lead, not like today's graphite, "lead" pencils. Later, a goose quill and ink were introduced to students who spent many hours learning to spread the ink over the letters evenly without splotches. It's no wonder penmanship became an important subject in so many of these schools.

Give honor to thy parents due.

The following set of activities can be done as individual projects, but if combined will produce several items with a distinct colonial look to them. If students succeed in creating a hornbook or primer pages, you may want to have them share these with the kindergarten or first grade classes. Make the proper arrangements and allow your students to be the teachers in a small group setting using the materials they have prepared.

In developing the writing activities, you may want students to imitate some of the nuances of colonial writing. These included using a "y" instead of a "th" when writing the word "the." Thus the sentence "Read the Bible," would appear "Read ye Bible." The lower case "s" also had a different appearance. In some texts it appears to look almost identical to the lower case "f." The slight difference is in the placement of the crossing line (f). In other texts the letter "s" has an elongated (f) appearance which is also sometimes mistaken for a peculiar f. Thus, words might look like this: fir$f$t (first), feffion (session) or like this: $f$mall (small), fa$f$t (fast).

Making a Hornbook

Making a modern-day hornbook can be fun for students. It requires little in the way of special materials and will produce an object students can actually use with younger children.

Materials:

corrugated cardboard about 7-1/2" x 11"
a piece of paper (lined or not) about 5" x 6"
plastic wrap or a two-liter, transparent, soda pop container
colored construction paper or half inch thick ribbon
tacks
white glue or rubber cement (masking tape optional)

Procedure:

1. Have students prepare the writing on the 5" x 6" piece of paper. It should contain the alphabet in both upper and lower case, a set of two-letter syllables, and finally, it should have a verse or sentence of some sort.

ABCDEFGHIJKLMNO
PQRSTUVWXYZ
abcdefghijklmno
pqrstuvwxyz
ab eb ib ob ub
ba be bi bo bu
The quick brown Fox
Jumped over the Lazy
Dog's Back. 1234567890

Hornbook (continued)

2. The process of preparing a hornbook may take time. The final copy should be printed, have correctly formed letters, and be extremely neat. Practice will be needed. Students may want to add a border to this work.
3. Cut a hornbook shape (a paddle with a handle) out of the corrugated cardboard. The paddle part will be about 8-1/2" x 7-1/2". The handle will be 2-1/2" x 1-1/2".
4. Glue or rubber cement the finished paper to the paddle of the hornbook and center it.
5. Cut a piece of plastic wrap or a piece of plastic out of a two-liter soda pop container (see illustration below) that equals 5-1/2" x 6-1/2".
6. Cut construction paper or ribbon into strips. Two strips will be 1/2" x 7-1/2" and two strips will be 1/2" x 6-1/2".
7. Using the construction paper or ribbon as a border, tack the plastic down over the paper. The plastic from the soda pop bottle may be too curly to stay put. If the tacks are not sufficient, tape it down with masking tape and put the border over the tape. If all else fails, put brass brads right through the border, plastic, and cardboard and bend them over on the other side.

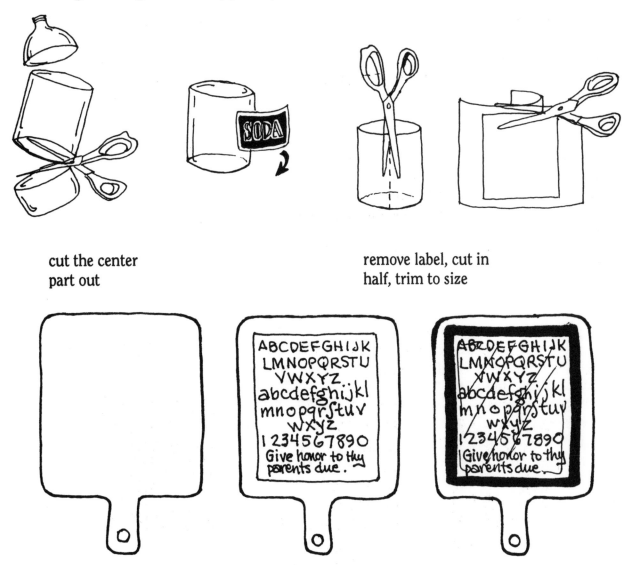

cut the center
part out

remove label, cut in
half, trim to size

ACTIVITY *Primer Pages*

To reinforce the learning of the alphabet and to give students practice reading, the *New England Primer* included rhymed verses with illustrations like the ones on page 71. Two-thirds of these verses related to the Bible such as the following:

P – *Peter* denies
His Lord and cries.

R – *Rachel* doth mourn
for her first born.

U – *Uriah's* beauteous Wife
Made David seek his life.

W – *Whales* near the Cay
God's Voice obey.

Another part of the primer was a page entitled "The Dutiful Child's Promises." It included moralistic advice and was designed to give students practice in reading and writing as well as to reinforce proper moral behavior. A sample of these promises includes:

I will honour the King.
I will honour my Father & Mother.
I will Obey my Superiours.
I will Love my Friends.
I will hate no Man.

Purpose:

To develop poetic rhyme and moral advice that relates to the students' world today.

Cooperative Grouping:

This project can be done individually, in pairs, or as an entire class project. It also works very well if students are put into cooperative groups of four to six with each group producing a book. Each group will be responsible for working together to create the verses and the list of "dutiful promises." Group members will further need to divide the labor of writing, illustrating, and bordering among them. Spend time helping students get organized by listing the jobs involved in completing this project so that they can decide how to use their resources to complete each step.

Procedure:

1. Organize cooperative groups as described above.
2. Allow students time to develop the pages for the primer according to a schedule. You may or may not want to have students use the different formation for the letter "s" described on page 72, or the spelling of "ye" for "the."
3. Have students create a cover that includes the word "Primer" (e.g., The Parkview School Primer) with a cover design on thicker construction paper. One week is usually enough time to complete the writing when done in periods of 45 minutes per day.
4. Bind the books with yarn, brads, or staples.
5. Arrange for small groups of students to present their books to a younger grade such as first or second.

ACTIVITY   *Writing With a Quill Pen*

Once colonial children had learned their letters and how to read, many were finished with literacy training. Some did go on to more advanced study, and that involved learning how to write in ink with a quill pen. This was no easy task. First it involved practicing with a sharpened stick and ink. Students had to learn how much ink to get on the tip and how lightly to press to make thin, graceful, legible letters with a minimum number of ink splotches. A blotting pad was always available when too much ink was let out on the paper at one time.

Purpose:

To write using the same implements that colonial students used.

Materials:

turkey feathers (purchased in craft shops) or sharpened sticks
washable ink such as the kind used in art (water soluble as not to ruin anyone's clothes)
paper towels for blotting and clean-up
paper
small cups in which to put the ink (e.g., pill dispensing cups)
paint shirts (oversized shirts students wear to protect their clothing)

Procedure:

1. Demonstrate and go over class rules for using ink.
2. Distribute feathers or sticks.
3. Pour ink into small cups about half full.
4. Have students practice writing the alphabet with the ink; have paper towels available for blotting.
5. If students get proficient, they may want to use this technique in designing their hornbook or primer.

ACTIVITY *Making Homemade Ink*

The colonists relied mostly on indigo ink for their writing. Indigo ink is made from the indigo plant. Indigo became one of the chief crops of the southern colonies as a result of its demand.

Because of the short supply of this ink and/or its cost many households used a homemade variety of ink. A recipe that uses walnut shells follows.

When doing these two activities, have students wear protective clothing such as paint shirts. These are dyes and will stain permanently.

Purpose:

To witness the chemical change involved in transferring chemicals found naturally in plants into liquid dyes.

walnut shells (black walnuts are best)
sauce pan
heat source such as a hot plate
water
salt and vinegar
cheese cloth
glass jar

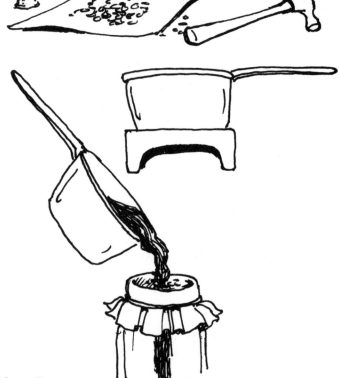

Procedure:

1. Crush the walnut shells into very small pieces.
2. Put the crushed shells in the sauce pan, cover with water, bring to a boil, and simmer until the liquid is deep brown.
3. Sprinkle salt into the liquid and add two or three tablespoons of vinegar to "set" the color.
4. Strain the liquid through a cheese cloth into the glass jar.
5. Allow the ink to cool before using it.

FOLLOW-UP ACTIVITY *Making Dyes*

Colonists soon found many plants that yielded dyes that would "set" as permanent color. Among these were iris flowers, goldenrod, various berries such as pokeberry, and barks from red oak and hickory trees. You can allow students to experiment with these and other plants they gather by following the same procedure outlined above. Have pieces of white cloth available to try out their dyes.

You may also want students to record their results as they experiment with different dyes. Have them record what color the plant produces, how long it takes to produce, whether it sets naturally or needs the salt and vinegar.

Apprenticeship

Reading and writing were seen as valuable by the colonists, but the real education of children involved preparing them for the work they would be doing the rest of their lives. As the colonial center moved to cities and towns, boys no longer needed to learn the business of agriculture. Whereas girls still were educated in domestic ways, boys might now learn the trade or craft of their fathers. This might mean becoming a blacksmith, joiner (cabinet maker), printer, cooper (barrel maker), whitesmith (tin worker), cobbler, or tailor.

Since families were large, some households could not support several boys learning the trade of their father. In these cases, boys were apprenticed to other craftsmen who would keep them in room and board for a period of four to seven years. During that time the apprentice agreed not to leave or marry. He was expected to serve his master and in return he learned the trade or craft. Girls might also be apprenticed to learn domestic chores. Apprenticing began for some children at the early age of six, but waiting until a child had reached adolescence was more common.

Apprentices were often treated as part of the family. They had their own bed in the "master's" home, ate meals with the master's family, celebrated holidays with that family, and in many cases ended up marrying into the family.

During their apprenticeship they did all tasks required. This included all sorts of cleaning, hauling, and mostly the hard labor the master would not have to do himself. Much of the work might not even relate to the skill the apprentice was learning, but that was all part of the arrangement.

Apprentices might be treated very well or might be treated poorly. Laws helped to protect the apprentice from a harsh master who would whip the apprentice too much or deny the apprentice life's necessities or the agreed upon learning. On the other hand, these same laws protected the master from a thieving apprentice or one who would not do as instructed. Both parties could be forced to appear before a judge and if found guilty would have to pay reparation and perhaps even submit to a punishment.

As mentioned above girls could be apprenticed as easily as boys. The difference was in the type of tasks they were expected to learn. A colonial woman had to be able to clean wool, dye it, spin it into yarn, weave it into cloth, and make clothing. She had meals to make, soap and candles to make, quilting, drying herbs and flowers, and all other domestic chores. Parents of higher social standing might also want their child to learn to be a lady. In this case she might also receive lessons in proper sitting and standing, playing musical instruments, dance, and embroidery.

Samplers were projects developed by mistresses to help young ladies learn their stitches. They typically would include some prayer, saying, or advice with an illustration to go with what was written. Today, samplers have become a part of Americana found in many households. In colonial times typical sayings might have included:

"This is my Sampler,
  Here you see,
  What care my Lady,
  Took of me."

"Mary Jackson is my name,
  I live in Massachusetts.
  Boston is my dwelling place,
  My King I do honour.

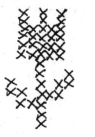

"In prosperity friends will be plenty,
  But in adversity not one in twenty."

"Twenty-first of Maye,
  Was our Wedding Daye."

The alphabet and numbers might also be included. The following activity will allow students to design a sampler that reflects today's society.

Purpose:

To create original sampler designs.

Materials:

graph paper (1/2 inch or 1/4)
pencil
colored pencils optional
colored construction paper

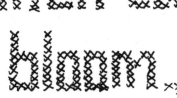

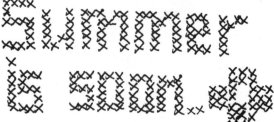

When tulips bloom,
Summer is soon.

Procedure:

1. On separate paper have students plan their sayings and designs.
2. On graph paper have them create the illustrations and sayings by X-ing each block with regular or colored pencils.
3. Mat these with colored construction paper.

CHAPTER SEVEN
Health and Medicine

Improvements

By today's standards of medical technology, the practice of medicine just 60 years ago was inadequate. For example, 60 years ago penicillin was not readily available; a simple cut in the rose garden could lead to a deadly infection, polio still afflicted many, and tuberculosis testing and open heart surgery did not exist. A quarantine sign was not an uncommon sight in cities and towns. Infant inoculations against typhoid, measles, mumps, rubella, and diphtheria were not generally practiced let alone mandated for entry into school as such inoculations are now. Sports medicine did not exist, nor did the number and types of specialists that populate the world of medicine today. General practitioners and country doctors abounded. Sulphur drugs were considered modern, reliable technology whereas today they are prohibited. Hospitals were quiet zones by law.

That was 60 years ago. Now, imagine the state of medical practice (or mispractice) 360 years ago. It was a time of bleeding patients, of avoiding fresh air and bathing, of being treated with animal excrement, of unstoppable epidemics, of no hospitals, and of virtually no licensing of physicians.

Mortality in the Colonies

Considering the living conditions, the lack of knowledge, and the many beliefs that bordered on superstition it is a wonder that any of the colonists survived. Indeed, many did not. One hundred and forty-four colonists left England in 1606 to establish Jamestown. Only 105 survived the voyage. Of those 105, only 38 survived the first year. Half of the 102 pilgrims that sailed on the *Mayflower* died within the first six months. Even after Plymouth was well established, one-fourth of the people died before the age of 21. Before 1650 the mortality rate per year in Chesapeake was as high as 80 percent. Epidemics, however, did not allow the early mortality rates that were due to poor living conditions to ebb. A diphtheria epidemic that occurred in New England from 1735 to 1737 resulted in 5,000 deaths.

One couple lost 8 children in one week during that epidemic. The famous Puritan minister Cotton Mather lost 5 of his family members in two weeks to a measles epidemic. Of his 15 children, only 2 lived longer than he. Judge Sewell had 14 children, but 5 died in infancy and 5 more died before the age of 30.

These statistics and incidences can be viewed as typical or as aberrations. In fact, they are a little of both. The truly amazing thing about the general state of health in the colonies during the seventeenth and eighteenth centuries is that it was largely better than that found in Europe. Epidemics were just as rampant in England. Famines were common throughout Europe but did not exist in colonies after the initial "starving times" of first settlements. Colonists were generally better nourished and better able to ward off diseases than their European counterparts.

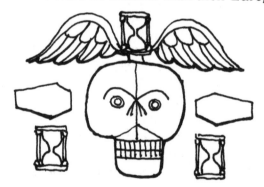

ACTIVITY   *Estimating Mortality Rates Then and Now*

In Philadelphia in 1793 a yellow fever epidemic killed 10 percent of the population. Well-populated cities such as Philadelphia were particularly susceptible to epidemics because of close living conditions and poor sanitation.

If such an epidemic were to occur today in a major city like Boston, over 50,000 people would die. In New York City over 700,000 lives would be claimed. Have students look up the populations of major cities in the United States and using the 10 percent proportion, have them figure out what the mortality rate would be if epidemics were allowed to claim 10 percent of the population. Individual students can be assigned specific cities and the results can be condensed into a bar graph to dramatize the impact of these statistics. A bulletin board can be developed using this graph.

Illnesses

The leading killers in colonial America were smallpox, yellow fever, dysentery, malaria, diphtheria, cholera, scarlet fever, measles, influenza, typhoid fever, and whooping cough. Conspicuously missing from this list are today's killers of cancer and heart disease probably due to the fact that these diseases were often diagnosed as something else. Also, both of these diseases develop more among the elderly, and fewer people in the colonies lived to the ages they do today.

For many colonists the voyage by ship was an infestation nightmare. Fresh drinking water was put in barrels at the beginning of the trip but often became tainted by the middle of the voyage. Cooking food was possible in sandboxes but only during good weather. A limited diet of salted meats and cheese served to debilitate a traveler even further. Often food spoiled but was eaten anyway.

Cramped quarters were the norm. Some captains insisted that passengers remain below deck. Seasickness prevailed, and if any serious illness afflicted one passenger it quickly passed to the others. The voyage lasted from 45 days to three months depending on the weather. In that time colonists became physically worn down and then had to confront new diseases that faced them in the colonies.

Illnesses followed certain cyclical patterns. In New England March was known as the sickly season. The long winter months of limited food, drafty living conditions, and poor hygiene took their toll. Specifically, a diet heavy with salted meats and corn created vitamin deficiencies. Seventeenth century thinking held that raw vegetables were unhealthy and this thinking resulted in a severe lack of vitamin intake. Scurvy, beriberi, and pellagra were all diseases caused by dietary deficiencies.

In the southern colonies, spring and summer brought malaria, "the great debilitator." Malaria could kill its victims, but more often than not it left them in a permanently weakened condition. As a result, pneumonia, influenza, or other diseases were better able to flourish in these patients.

Beliefs regarding personal hygiene that we hold strange today also contributed to the development of illness in the colonies. Held over from England was a distrust of water. It was not the beverage of choice. Alcoholic beverages were more common for everyone, even children. Bathing was viewed with equal suspicion. One account by a Quaker woman mentions that when she showered while visiting a friend in the city (showers were new by the end of the eighteenth century), it was the first time in 28 years that she had been wet all over.

The growth of cities promoted illness. Rubbish was often indiscriminately thrown out the doors. At one time hogs were allowed to roam the streets to scavenge through the refuse which only added to the unsanitary conditions. In the cities poor sewage often led to contaminated water supplies or areas of standing water that encouraged mosquito (and thus malaria) development. Perhaps one element that most contributed to the prevention of epidemics in the early colonies was the fact that people were isolated on farms.

 ACTIVITY   *Growing Microorganisms*

In the early colonial times no one believed that illnesses were caused by microorganisms. In the mideighteenth century, due to the studies done in Europe, inoculations began to catch a foothold, but many viewed them with great doubt. In some cities laws were actually passed preventing inoculations, and in some towns near riots developed when it was learned that someone had received an inoculation (thus endangering everyone's life).

Purpose:

To demonstrate the abundance of microorganisms present in our environment.

Materials:

tomato soup	water	large spoon
5 containers	plastic wrap	masking tape and pen
hot plate	rubber bands	

Procedure:

1. Sterilize the containers and spoon.
2. Add water to the tomato soup and bring it to a boil
3. Add several spoonfuls of soup to the first container. Immediately cover with plastic wrap and secure with rubber band. With masking tape label the container.
4. Follow the same procedure for the next four containers but for each add the following:
   container 2 – Expose soup to air for 30 minutes before covering and labeling.
   container 3 – After soup has cooled, have a student stir the soup.
   container 4 – Stir the soup with a pen or pencil.
   container 5 – Have a student spit, cough, or sneeze into the soup.
5. Put containers in a warm, dark place and chart the growth of mold daily. Students can record data and draw conclusions about the presence of microorganisms in their environment. Relate this to the likelihood of diseases being transmitted in a colonial city given the above information.

The Healers

The number of physicians available to New England colonists is surprisingly high. This may have been due to the fact that requirements for calling oneself a physician can best be described as loose. In England the medical profession had three tiers. The physician, who was allowed to be called "doctor," specialized in diagnosis of illness and prescribing cures. Surgeons, who were called "mister," were actually a step lower on the scale. They performed surgeries but were thought of as craftsmen. Apothecaries were today's pharmacists. A patient might be required to visit any or all three of these men. In colonial America, this three-tiered system quickly broke down because the people were so spread out. One man had to perform the function of all three.

Many American doctors were self-trained or had served as apprentices under practitioners who were self-trained or apprenticed. Only five percent of the doctors in America in 1776 held degrees in medicine. Licensing was not required and some of the most notable physicians in colonial history, such as the Reverend Gershom Bulkeley, received their licenses only after years of practice and received them as honorary degrees. Most educated men received some sort of medical knowledge in their schooling. Since ministers were the most likely candidates to receive such an education, it was natural that the clergy took on the role of physicians in colonial villages and townships.

The isolated nature of so many farms throughout the southern and coastal colonies made the development of folk medicine prevalent in those areas. Any individual who had lived long enough might develop a reputation as a healer or "doctor." Unlike apprenticed physicians, these individuals relied on "tried and true" methods for cure. Their medical bags would contain a startling supply of dried herbs, barks, flowers, and a large dose of personal experience.

Because of the hit-and-miss nature of most treatments, many colonists formed a very dubious opinion of the medical establishment during the Colonial Period. For instance, Thomas Jefferson said that he looked up to see if buzzards were circling overhead whenever he saw several physicians gathering. In 1757 it was said that "quacks" were as numerous as locusts in Egypt. The trust level of physicians throughout New England was such that unless personal experience had taught otherwise, people waited until dire need prompted them to call a physician.

Today, public trust of the medical profession should be much higher, but is it? Many people today still wait until the last minute before seeing a doctor. You can have your class explore opinions of their school or community regarding the medical profession by having them design an opinion poll.

Purpose:

To experience the gathering and interpreting of primary source data. To speculate on the changing attitude of the public toward the medical profession.

Procedure:

1. Target the Audience and Subject.

   As a class or in small groups have students decide what kind of information they want to gather. They must answer questions such as: Who is our target audience? What do we want to learn through our survey?

   With respect to the second question, students need to decide whether they want to learn about the audience's attitude toward doctors, hospitals, treatments, or the medical profession in general.

   Finally, have them decide on three to five main questions that they want answered such as:

   How much do people trust the judgment of their doctors?
   Do people have regular medical check-ups?
   How long do people wait before going to see a doctor?

2. Construct the Survey Questions.

   For each question the class wants answered, design one or two survey questions. The questions can be one of three types:

   Yes/No questions–Do you believe doctors receive an adequate training to
        practice medicine?

   Quality questions–Please rate how much you trust a hospital to provide adequate
        care for you (and your family).

   Open-ended questions–How long would you wait before seeing a doctor if you
        became ill?

3. Administer the Survey to the Target Audience.

   Each student can be equipped with X number of surveys and be responsible for gathering data.

4. Analyze the Results and Draw Conclusions.

   Depending on the question type, students can tabulate yes and no responses, tally scores and average, or read and interpret open-ended questions. Allow students to discuss these findings in small groups with each group drawing its own conclusions. The conclusions may prompt more investigation. Share the results with an interested group.

The Cures

Diagnosis of ailments in the sixteenth and seventeenth centuries relied on the most recent medical knowledge. For trained physicians that meant an understanding of the humors: heat, dryness, moistness, and cold. If the doctor decided that an illness arose from heat, it was treated with cold; if the illness was the result of moistness, the patient had to be dried. Balance was the key. However, attempts to regain this balance often resulted in remedies that seemed worse than the illness. Chief among these was bloodletting or phlebotomy. Many a patient was allowed to bleed to purge the body of its ill humors. One physician was said to have performed so much bloodletting on one patient that he cured a man of the disease known as his wife. Purging did not just mean bloodletting. People were given concoctions that caused sweating, diarrhea, and vomiting. Purging may have worked in some instances, but in others it may have fatally weakened the patient.

Home remedies abounded and produced some very strange practices. Pills made of cotton or sugar and "sallet oyl" were prescribed for smallpox. Gout was treated with a poultice of boiled onion. A plaster of cow dung boiled in milk was applied to frozen limbs. One general rule of thumb is that the remedy be as awful tasting, smelling, or feeling as the disease. Such remedies may not have cured anyone, but they surely kept others away from the diseased person and thus may have prevented contagion.

Not all home remedies were quackery. Some of the first remedies in the colonies were handed down by the native Americans who relied on herbs and roots found in nature, many of which worked. Digitalis, used widely today in medicines, was developed by an eighteenth century physician who relied on a folk medicine employing foxglove leaves.

Below is a list of medically related topics that students can investigate. Some will require traditional book-type investigations. Others may require the use of periodicals. Still others may require that students use less traditional investigative techniques such as interviews. Discuss each investigative method with students before assigning any of them. The investigations can be done individually or in small groups.

1. What herbs or roots have been scientifically found to have healing properties?

2. How many "old wives' tales" related to the causes of illness and/or healing can you uncover? Interview people in your family, neighborhood, and community to get the information. Keep a journal of these old wives' tales. Discuss which ones seem impossible and which seem plausible.

3. The story of the discovery of penicillin is fascinating. It was an accident that led to this life-saving drug. Research the story behind penicillin. Interview a doctor or pharmacist to find out all the ways it is used today.

4. Develop a list of rules for long life. Interview people who have lived long and healthy lives and make a journal of their advice. Research what medical science says contributes to living a long life and compare it to the journal entries.

5. What do doctors do to become doctors? Research the education and training needed to become a doctor. Interview a doctor to find out what character traits she or he thinks are necessary to become and stay an effective practitioner.

6. How many different specialties are there? Contact a hospital or look in the Yellow Pages to find out how many specialist areas there are in medicine. Which ones are the most recent? Interview someone in the medical profession to find out whether general practitioners exist anymore. Are general practitioners obsolete?

7. Investigate some of the alternative medical treatments such as acupuncture, hypnosis, and faith healing. Develop a survey to find out what your community or neighborhood thinks about these forms of medicine.

CHAPTER EIGHT
Recreation, Sports, and Holidays

Puritan Attitude

Fun and frivolity were certainly not exported to the colonies with some of its first settlers, the Puritans. Rather, these activities were viewed as an immoral and shameful waste of time. When the Puritans came to the colonies, they brought with them the desire to purify a religion, the Church of England, that they thought had become corrupt. Part of this purification meant turning people's minds from pleasures. Pleasures, they believed, kept people from their one and only goal, that of glorifying God on earth.

This is not to say that the Puritans sought only to deprive themselves of worldly enjoyment. They certainly sought to enjoy the comforts of life brought about by their efforts in work and business. Overindulgence, which they believed took the place of God on earth, was their enemy. Material wealth was not bad, but the love of material wealth was. Holidays were fine unless they were celebrated in a way that turned one's focus from God to one's self. Leisure time was thought of as a trap of idleness laid by the devil.

Since so much work needed to be done, it may not even have been necessary to have a Puritan attitude toward enjoyable diversions. The sheer amount of work would easily have kept most early colonists from engaging in recreational activities. Thus, the Puritan attitude as well as the circumstances had a tremendous effect in shaping holidays and recreation in the colonies.

Holidays

The celebration of holidays in England had been evolutionary. The number, type, and manner of celebration had evolved over hundreds of years. When people arrived in the colonies, any ideas that they had of continuing these celebratory traditions never materialized because many English holidays were tied to harvesting times in England. In the colonies harvesting times were not only different from those in England, they were also different between northern and southern colonies. When the New Englander was harvesting, the southern colonist was just beginning to plant his tobacco crop.

In New England the Puritans did away with the celebration of Christmas and other holidays observed by the Church of England. In fact, fines were levied and punishments were dispensed to anyone doing anything on Christmas Day that might be interpreted as a celebration. Shops had to remain open and a full day's work was expected. In the South, however, the Church of England was the religion of choice so the colonists there continued to observe it as well as Easter in the traditional manner. Throughout the seventeenth century not one holiday or celebration united the people of the colonies. It was up to colonists of individual regions to devise their own holidays and celebrations.

One necessity for the early colonists was the ability for a village to defend itself. Every able-bodied man was expected to take part in military drills. This was called "mustering the troops," and soon a day was set aside for this drill and practice known as *Muster Day*. This day evolved in some areas as a holiday that included drinking in the tavern (if there was one), games, races, athletic contests, and shooting matches. This holiday was popular well into the eighteenth century but died out as a standing militia took the place of men able to muster for defense at a moment's notice. Another civic holiday included court day, when everyone would gather in the village to hear cases brought before judges. Election day was still another time in which people gathered thus bringing about reason for festivity. Finally, it was usually only proper to honor the King of England with a day in celebration of his birthday.

Another truly American holiday that caught on was Thanksgiving. In England harvest celebrations were common, so in the colonies it did not take long to establish similar celebrations. The first Thanksgiving involving the Pilgrims and native Americans was celebrated in the autumn of 1621. In the Massachusetts Bay Colony, it was celebrated first on July 8, 1630, to give thanks for the safe arrival of John Winthrop to New England. As mentioned above, southern colonists had a different timetable for Thanksgiving owing to the difference in their harvest time. Therefore, a harvest celebration or Thanksgiving was established in various regions at different times.

As colonial city life became established, so too did the taverns. Soon gentlemen were forming clubs or fraternal organizations often in honor of the patron saints of their countries, St. George, St. Patrick, or St. Andrew. Each of these clubs, in turn, would set aside the patron saint's feast day as a day of celebration.

At first a few strictly English holidays were observed in some regions such as Guy Fawke's Day, celebrated in honor of the man who plotted to blow up Parliament. As time went on, however, colonists devised their own days of celebration. Commencement Day at Harvard became a day of celebration in that area alone. Victories during the French and Indian War led to holidays in other settlements.

ACTIVITY   *Holidays for Everyone*

Today's list of holidays celebrated by Americans may be longer than that of the colonists. In addition to national holidays (which now help to unite our country), there are many cultural and religious holidays. Recognizing the diversity of holidays celebrated by Americans helps us to appreciate the diversity of the American people.

Purpose:

To become aware of the national holidays that all Americans celebrate and how we celebrate them. To investigate some of the ethnic and religious holidays celebrated by the American people.

Procedure:

1. As a class make a list of national holidays that all Americans celebrate or recognize. This list may include other events that are not official holidays but are widely recognized as important days in our country's history such as D-Day. Then create another list of ethnic/religious holidays that only specific groups of Americans celebrate. Use a calendar to help in the composition of this list.
2. Divide students into groups of two to four.
3. Each group will investigate one holiday from each list. In its investigation each group is to find out the history behind the day and some of the different ways it is celebrated.
4. Each group will be responsible for first, developing a posterboard visual aid that illustrates what they learned about that holiday and second, for presenting the information to the class.

Feasting and holidays went together in colonial times as they do today. When people got together, it was natural to include eating. A holiday feast might include foods that were not usually eaten on a day-to-day basis. Ginger snaps were one of these treats. They were baked for company and for holidays.

The following recipe contains some ingredients such as brown sugar, molasses, and spices that were hard for colonists to come by, thus making them a treat for special occasions. Students may follow the recipe in class or at home. A toaster oven or regular oven is the only requirement that may make it difficult to do this in school.

Materials:

mixing bowls	measuring cups and spoons	spatula
cookie sheet	clean, flat surface	toaster oven

Ingredients:

3/4 cup butter	3-3/4 cups all purpose flour
2 cups sugar	1-1/2 tsps. baking soda
2 beaten eggs	2 or 3 tsps. ginger
1/2 cup molasses	1/2 tsp. cinnamon
2 tsp. cider vinegar	1/4 tsp. cloves or nutmeg (optional)

Procedure:

1. Soften the butter and cream with sugar.
2. To this stir in eggs, molasses, and vinegar.
3. In a separate bowl mix the flour, baking soda, ginger, and cinnamon (add optional cloves or nutmeg).
4. Mix all ingredients until blended well.
5. Form into one-inch balls and place on cookie sheet.
6. Bake at 325° for 12 minutes.

Europeans soon found that the temperate climate of New England lent itself well to the growing of apples. Apple orchards quickly became common on many New England farms. This fruit stored well in the winter and provided a wonderful break from the bland and monotonous foods of winter. The first, the apple fritter, was a dessert treat that was served at harvest festivals and fairs.

In making apple fritters with students be sure to set up safety rules since you will be working with hot oil. Butter knives can be used for peeling and cutting. The activity is safe but students may have a difficult time making good rings. Slices are fine. Using an old-fashioned apple peeler may not be colonial, but it is handy.

Materials:

butter knives
measuring cups and spoons
mixing bowls
small pot or pan
frying pan
hot plate
spatula
paper towels
fork

Ingredients:

5-8 apples
1 tbs. melted butter
2 large eggs
3/4 cup milk
1-1/2 cups all purpose flour
pinch of salt
2 tbs. sugar
vegetable oil
powdered sugar (optional)

Procedure:

1. Peel and core the apples with knives.
2. Cut the apples into rings or slices about 1/4-inch thick.
3. Beat the eggs; add milk and beat again.
4. Melt the butter and set aside; mix the flour, salt, and sugar lightly; add melted butter and blend together. This batter should be thick.
5. Heat a little less than 1/2 inch of oil in the frying pan.
6. Dip the apple rings/slices into batter and fry them turning once so that they are golden brown on both sides. Add oil as necessary.
7. Take the fritters out of the oil and place them on paper towels to drain and cool. Sprinkle with powdered sugar (though not a colonial step).

Colonists did not especially like to drink water. They did because little else was available, but as time went by and villages grew, many replacements for water were developed. One such replacement was apple cider. It was relatively easy to make, needing no fermentation like wine nor special grains like beer. It also kept amazingly well. If it did spoil, the resultant vinegar was used in baking.

Coming from England, the first colonists liked hot drinks. At fairs and during holidays taking simple apple cider and making it into a hot spiced drink was very simple.

Materials:

hot plate
large pot with a lid
measuring spoons and cups
cheesecloth with string or strainer
ladle
cups for serving hot liquid

Ingredients:

1 gallon apple cider
1 cup brown sugar
2 tsp. whole cloves
1 tbs. all spice
3 sticks of cinnamon

Procedure:

1. Pour the cider into the pot.
2. Add the brown sugar and stir to dissolve as much as possible.
3. Put spices in cheesecloth and tie with string; or if you are going to use a strainer, then just drop them all into the pot.
4. Cover the pot and bring to a boil. Simmer on low for 20 minutes (or less if you want less of a spicy taste).
5. Remove the cheesecloth bag or pour the drink through the strainer.
6. Ladle out a taste of it for each student. This recipe makes about 16 full cups. If you use a 5-oz. paper cup, you will get about 24 servings. Increase the recipe proportionately if you need more.

Although the first colonists, specifically the Puritans, disdained all form of revelry and decoration at Christmas, colonial immigrants from other countries did not. German, Dutch, and Scandinavian settlers that inhabited the Middle Colonies brought with them a rich tradition of holiday celebration. The yule log, a variety of decorations, and a multitude of meals and beverages were traditions that came from the Old Country and are still today a part of many households. For example, the Swedish made birds out of wool and used them for decoration. In the South the traditional English wassail bowl was kept filled. Among German colonists an evergreen tree was cut, brought indoors, and decorated.

The tree decorated by colonists would look distinctly different from today's lighted and ornamented trees. Candles illuminated the trees (a practice so hazardous that it was done only once on Christmas Eve). Homemade decorations adorned the boughs. Among these decorations was the colonial version of garland.

Below is a recipe for a garland made of popcorn and berries. The berries that the colonists used would have been whatever was available at that time of year. This recipe calls for cranberries which is a likely berry used by colonists. Cranberries were found throughout New England in a bog-like environment. Their dark red fruit matured late in the season, and the cranberry stayed preserved a remarkably long time after it had been picked. The cranberry was also a favorite in the making of jams, jellies, and sauces used during this holiday season. Popcorn would also have been natural material available for a garland. Corn had already been harvested and dried by this time of the year. The variety of corn that makes popcorn was stored and used for any special occasion.

Materials:

unpopped corn
fresh, hard cranberries
bowls
heavy duty thread
small buttons
needles
scissors

Procedure:

1. Pop the corn and allow it to cool.
2. Thread the needle and put a large knot at the other end.
3. First, string a button to prevent the popcorn or berries from coming off that end.
4. Begin stringing popcorn and berries in any pattern you wish.
5. Strings may need to be shorter than you wish since the weight makes it possible for them to break. You can connect several strings using a button between each one.

Recreation and Sports

The Puritans certainly had a profound influence on colonial recreation and leisure as did the new seasonal patterns. Within one generation, however, colonists had begun to create their own diversions. The amount of work necessary on a farm made everyday recreation unimaginable. Holidays, fairs, political events, or even a trip into the village became times for games and sports.

Each region allowed these social gatherings to develop naturally. Town meetings in the North and court days in the South were times when people gathered for political reasons but allowed the gathering to become social. Games and sports would spontaneously arise on such occasions. Where the Puritans rejected gatherings for the reason of pure enjoyment, they saw nothing wrong in combining work and pleasure. Thus, events such as husking bees, quilting bees, and house raisings became peculiarly American activities.

Southern colonists first adapted their environment to recreation. Hunting and fishing, once an activity of necessity, soon became a leisure activity among the plantation owners. Horse racing also caught on in the South and spread to the other colonies. In Virginia the raising of horses for racing became a passion among some of the gentry who imported pure-blooded horses from Europe. In Rhode Island pacers became well-known. Throughout the colonies clubs that held regular racing events were formed.

Gambling and gaming were carried over from England. Card games were played by both men and women. In the New England colonies such activities were, of course, soundly discouraged by both religion and law. In the coastal colonies and southern colonies, however, any gathering of people could lead to a game of dice or cards. Gambling on the horses and roosters was also natural as was the betting on athletic contests that might arise during fairs.

Other games and sports brought from England included bowling on the village green. In it a single white ball, called a jack, was placed at one end of the green and a team tried to carefully place all its bowls (slightly egg-shaped balls) around it. Ninepins, the precursor of today's bowling, also developed. In the North sled riding became a sport enjoyed by children from 8 to 18.

Music, dance, and drama developed in the colonies in different stages. Of course, in Puritan New England such diversions were discouraged unless it could be found that the practice of them served to glorify God. Thus, as late as the American Revolution, Boston still banned performances on stage.

Music played on the violin, flute, and horns was typical of men while ladies developed their talents on the harpsichord or spinet. Dance also went through its own evolution. Sedate minuets gave way to much more active reels and jigs which characterized early colonial dance. Everywhere colonists adapted music and dance to fit their ever-changing culture.

ACTIVITY   *The Broadside*

The first music that people brought with them from Europe became what the colonists considered American music. English ballads, traditional French songs, and Dutch and German melodies all came together in America. Out of this mixture grew popular American songs. First among these popular songs was a type of political propaganda called the broadside. By the eighteenth century the one thing that all people loved to discuss when they got together was politics and political problems. When events occurred in one town, news of them quickly spread in the form of a song. Following an event such as the hanging of a pirate or a court judgment, words describing (or even parodying) the event were written to accompany a well-known tune. The words were quickly printed onto sheets and sold by street peddlers, sometimes within hours of the event. Only the words were printed since it was assumed everyone would already know the tune.

Colonists readily took to this unique combination of entertainment and communication. Eighteenth century taverns filled with men who found great enjoyment in singing about the latest current events.

As the colonists became more and more dissatisfied with English rule, the broadsides often took on a bitter, satirical edge. Some writers used them to encourage political dissent and rebellion. Samuel Adams saw the broadside as a political tool and even organized singing groups in Boston which would clearly voice their dissatisfaction with British rule.

ACTIVITY   *Writing a Broadside*

The tunes that were popular during colonial times are lost today except for what was written into a musical score at the end of the eighteenth century. One tune that all school children still sing, however, is "Yankee Doodle."

Using this tune as a base, have students write their own lyrics describing an American historical event. For example, Paul Revere's ride could start this way:

> Paul Revere, he galloped fast
> To shout and warn the people
> He'd seen the lights come flashing forth
> From yonder high church steeple.

The Boston Tea Party, the Stamp Act, and the landing at Plymouth can all be events that are put to this song. Students can then use this same song or perhaps an equally familiar one to describe a current event.

CHAPTER NINE
Crime and Punishment in the Colonies

Off to a Bad Start

When Jamestown was established in 1607, it was made up of a group of men with a common goal—to find and dig up the gold and silver that this new land had to offer. They did not know that the only gold available was iron pyrite or fool's gold. The Virginia Company sponsored the colony and solicited the help of men who were ill prepared for the hardships that awaited them. Upon arrival more time was spent digging and searching than establishing a proper colony.

The men were unwilling to do the work necessary to ensure their very survival. Proper housing was not erected. A food supply was not established. Even the location of Jamestown was obviously poor and supplied inadequate means for survival. Still, no one thought to move. The men were unable to defend themselves because few had had any training in military discipline. Furthermore, a number of them were "gentlemen" who had never done manual labor and were not about to start. As a result, within months the conditions in Jamestown were so bad that it was possible that no one in the colony would survive.

Law and Order in Jamestown

Under these circumstances John Smith took a leadership role and established routines and dictates that provided the foundation for a successful colony. His rules included a daily regimen that the men had to follow, a list of dos and don'ts along with a punishment for offenders. These rules became the first effective laws in the New World. Many of his laws could not be found in England because they were laws and punishments designed to provide for the survival of the colony.

For example, if a man were found guilty of malingering he was banished from the fort, a punishment that would surely lead to death as an individual alone in the wilderness. The message was clear; everyone had to pull his own weight. Theft was punishable by death since stealing (especially food items) jeopardized the life of all colony members. Excessive swearing or verbal complaining could result in a man having ice water poured down his sleeve that evening. This punishment resulted in an extremely uncomfortable experience that lasted all night since few of the men had a change of clothing. Everyone was expected to work and practice marching and mustering for defense, even the "gentlemen" who had accompanied the expedition. Failure to do so endangered the rest of the colony and was punished. Thus, the laws and punishments were dictated by the circumstances of the times.

The Puritan Form of Justice

When the Puritans left England, they had as their mission the establishment of a "City Upon a Hill" that would represent the true and proper manner in which Christianity would be carried out. They sought to purify their religion and to purify themselves to obtain God's grace. Basic to Puritanism were certain assumptions. One of the assumptions was that each person was a battleground between God and the devil, that people were forever struggling between God's law and the devil's temptations. Another assumption was the belief that people were inherently bad and that only through right living could anyone hope to attain salvation. These basic ideas formed the foundation for much of what became law throughout New England since it was the Puritans that established the first colonies of Massachusetts, Connecticut, Rhode Island, and New Hampshire.

Church law and state law intermingled in these colonies. It was illegal, for example, to enjoy any form of amusement that might lead one's thoughts from God. Thus, most forms of amusement (discussed in Chapter 8) were prohibited. So, too, was any form of idleness. Beachcombing was not allowed; and in many instances duck hunting was prohibited since if the hunter was not a good shot, he would be wasting resources and time.

JOHN SMITH

The laws of the Puritans were often tied to the Mosaic laws. Since long hair was deemed inappropriate by Biblical interpretation, frequent trips to the barber were expected. Overdressing was seen as a form of idol worship and was not allowed. Needless to say, swearing, sleeping during sermons, and failure to attend lecture were all punishable. Enforcing these laws, however, became a matter of choice from village to village, and by the beginning of the eighteenth century many colonists did not even know these laws existed.

Under such circumstances, ministers held an enormous amount of power in a community. To criticize one could easily result in a whipping, branding, or banishing as one schoolmaster experienced in New Haven, Connecticut. When transgressors got away with their crimes, many Puritans believed that a punishment from God was forthcoming. Thus, a drought or a violent storm was interpreted as God's hand taking control of rightful punishment. To help safeguard the community against such occurrences, snooping was encouraged. Quarreling between husband and wife in their own home might be reported and the couple forced to appear before a judge. Gossips could find their tongues pinched between the split end of a stick. People were even hired to check up on other people.

Although the Puritans viewed themselves as God's chosen who had been "winnowed" from the masses in England to start a new world in the wilderness, the fact is that many non-Puritan types joined them in New England. Not being a Puritan did not excuse a person from Puritan law. Many a man paid a fine for behaving in a way that was perfectly legal in his native England.

As in Jamestown, the Puritan form of law and order followed a system. This system, however, was not dictated by survival but by the moral judgment outlined by religious beliefs.

ACTIVITY   *A Book of Rules*

Purpose:

To examine many of the rules that govern students' daily lives and to analyze them in the context of their environment.

Procedure:

1. In small groups or as a class have students develop a list of rules that govern their daily lives in school.
2. Have the groups divide these rules into two categories: rules that apply only in school (such as not interrupting another student who is talking) and rules that apply both in school and outside school (such as rules against possession of drugs).
3. Groups will share these with the entire class to provide a master list from which everyone can work.
4. Allow groups to analyze each set of rules. This will include discussing and reaching consensus on what function each rule serves in the school environment.

    For example, a rule about not interrupting another student who is talking serves to promote learning in an environment where many people have a need to share ideas, opinions, and ask questions.
5. As a class discuss their analysis and decisions about what rules are most valuable and which ones are unneccessary. Create a master list. Compare to see which apply only in school and which apply out of the school environment. Is there a pattern? What conclusions can be drawn?
6. Finally, in their groups have students develop a list of rules they would want to see enforced in school. This list should be made into a book. Groups may also add rules that they feel are missing and would be for the better of the school. (Note: For this last one you will need to steer them away from rules all students would love to implement such as the "no homework" rule.)
7. Groups present their books in class and provide reasons for keeping, eliminating, or adding rules.

Note: This activity can be as simple or extended as you make it. Steps one through five can easily be accomplished in one class period. If you do steps six and seven, more class time will be needed.

Follow-up: Students can follow up this activity by individually analyzing the rules of their home environment. An individual written or oral report can follow.

Punishment by Humiliation

Puritan punishment was based on the premise that punishment should humiliate the transgressors so that they could see the error of their ways and change them. Most typical of colonial New England's penal code were the stocks and pillory. Stocks were heavy wooden frames with holes for securing the guilty party's ankles and sometimes wrists. The pillory was similar but was designed so that the person confined in it would be in a standing position with his or her head and wrists secured. The difference between the use of the two seems to have depended upon who was being punished. The pillory was reserved for members of the community with higher social standing, whereas the stocks were used for the lower class individuals. In any event being placed in the stocks was usually accompanied by the jeers of passing community members as well as an occasional rotten egg or vegetable. This was aided by the fact that the stocks and pillory were almost always placed by the meeting house where people would have more occasion to pass by.

Still another form of public humiliation might be to have the criminal wear something for a period of time. The most common thing to wear was a large letter that stood for the wrongdoing. Thus, a person who had stolen would wear a *T* for thief. A person who had sworn would wear a *B* for blasphemer while a drunkard wore a *D*. And, yes, an adulterer would wear a large *A* as was done in *The Scarlet Letter*. Still another form of humiliation might be to wear an iron collar or piece of rope about one's neck.

The ducking stool was still another common device of punishment. It was reserved for women and involved having a woman tied to a stool that was attached to a long pole with a fulcrum in the middle. Like a teeter-totter the stool was lowered into a lake or river with the woman attached. Gossiping and scolding one's husband were the crimes deserving of this punishment. The number of dunks depended on the decision of the judge. On occasion, however, a husband could save his wife by paying a fine although no records exist of how often this alternative was exercised.

FS-10139 Life as a Colonist

The length of this public humiliation would depend on the severity of the crime. Several hours to several days in the stocks or pillory were normal sentences. Wearing a letter might last months or even years. One man found guilty of rape was sentenced to wear an iron collar for the rest of his life.

Severity of Punishment

By today's standards such public humiliation would be seen as cruel and unusual punishment especially in a school. Compared to many of the alternative punishments available during colonial time, humiliation looked good.

The most popular form of punishment was whipping sometimes called *stripes* for the marks left on the victim. A whipping post usually stood next to the stocks and pillory as a grim reminder of what awaited people who engaged in more serious crimes or who chose to repeat their offenses. Theft, slander, criticism of authority, adultery, as well as many other lesser crimes could incur a whipping. A woman found guilty of emptying her dirty water in the streets received the lash. The number of stripes depended as usual on the crime. Twenty to forty was common. One case of a man receiving 117 was recorded. To add humiliation to the whipping the victim was sometimes forced to be tied to a cart and walk behind it as someone else followed and "whipped him through town."

The cruelty did not stop with whipping. A hot awl through the tongue was used occasionally for a person who preached falsely or spoke against the religion. Sometimes ears were cut off. A variation of wearing a letter was to have it branded onto the forehead or other body part.

One group of people that received more than their share of these punishments were the Quakers. The Quakers had beliefs other than those of the Puritans. In England they had developed a reputation for being a nuisance. This was because of their insistence on preaching their beliefs and criticizing others. They disrupted religious services and stood in town squares to tell one and all of the errors of their ways. Needless to say, the Puritans had little patience for this type of behavior. Quakers regularly were banished from Puritan villages. If they returned, as often they did because Quakers felt they had a mission to preach, they might experience whipping or branding. Some were executed.

Executions

Execution was also a form of punishment in the colonies. Hanging was among the most common form of death but burning was also used. Found guilty of insurrection, two men in New York were sentenced to be drawn and quartered, meaning that they were horribly mutilated as they were executed.

From this we may get an image that life in the colonies was precarious if not barbaric. All things being relative, however, punishment in the strictest New England town was not as bad as that found in England. Offenses such as petty larceny were punishable by death in England, but in reality the death sentence was rarely imposed in America. Murder was one crime that usually resulted in the death penalty. Piracy and treason also led to death. Prison terms, on the other hand, were uncommon. There were two reasons for this. First, everyone was needed to work and help support the colony. Putting someone in prison for theft or even indebtedness did not help the matter. The second reason was equally economic. Prisons were a drain on a colony's resources. Consequently, the colonists found punishments that were quick and inexpensive. Only when it was likely that a person might flee from debtors would he or she be locked up. Thieves were usually sentenced to pay back the person they stole from in labor or goods.

Colonial Punishment in Perspective

A good deal of tolerance also marked colonial law. People did not have the stomachs for frequent executions or brutal punishments. By the beginning of the eighteenth century few really harsh sentences were being handed out because public opinion was against it. In addition, a plea of the clergy was permitted in most courts; this plea was used for the severest crimes including murder. It allowed nearly any person who was a first-time offender to be granted dispensation if he or she agreed to be branded on the thumb. The brand served to identify a person as a former offender if arrested for subsequent crimes.

The law was and is an ever changing thing. Many laws developed by the first colonists were all but forgotten within 30 or 40 years. By the middle of the eighteenth century new laws were being written and enforced in answer to the blatant protests that many colonists had toward English rule. By today's standards many of the punishments were cruel and unusual but given the circumstances and environment the colonists thought them right and just.

It is fairly easy to sit and watch others pass judgment on someone and then criticize the judgment as too harsh or too lenient. As strict as colonial judges may have seemed to us, they knew that their decisions could be contested in the court of popular opinion. If a judgment were handed down that the village or colony thought unfit, pressure could be placed to have the judgment reversed or eventually to have the judge removed from office.

The following simulation provides a set of real situations taken from everyday life in colonial history. It will be up to the students to decide a fitting punishment.

Purpose:

To simulate the position of judge in a colonial court.

Procedure:

1. Set up teams of three. Each team will act as a set of judges.
2. Present one team with one of the situations listed on the page entitled "You Be the Judge." All situations are real. The actual punishment that was handed out during the colonial time has been added for your information. Students do not need to know any more information than is listed. It is their job to decide on a just punishment. It is not their job to decide on guilt or innocence. All situations involve people who were found guilty.
3. After being presented their situation and given time to discuss it, they will present their punishment to the class. The class will act as the members of the colonial town.
4. After judgment is given, the town will discuss and then vote as to whether the set of judges were just or not in the punishment they handed out. If the majority agrees, you can declare that these judges would have kept their jobs. If there is a great majority against their judgment, then you can explain that these judges would have lost their jobs.
5. After the first set is done, present another team with a different situation.

Variations:

1. Use this activity before presenting information on colonial crime and justice. It will provide a terrific contrast in what we view as fair and what colonists viewed as fair.
2. Present all situations to the judge teams at once and let them have time to discuss. Then have them present their situation, judgment, and rationale to the class. This will take less time than the above.

You Be the Judge

The following cases are taken from colonial history. The details have been given. After each case the punishment that was delivered is included.

1. A soldier was found guilty of killing a man during a riot in Boston. It was decided that the killing could have been avoided. This was part of what became known as the Boston Massacre. Punishment: The man was allowed to enter a plea of clergy. He was branded on the thumb and released.

2. In January a woman was found guilty of continually scolding her husband in public and embarrassing him.
   Punishment: Four dunks in the pond which was amended to one after the first dunk because of the weather.

3. In Virginia two men were found guilty of being Quakers and preaching publicly and creating a nuisance after being told to desist.
   Punishment: Given 32 lashes with a corded whip, pilloried, and banished.

4. A man was found guilty of stealing. He was unable to return the stolen goods and he had no property to give the man from whom he stole.
   Punishment: He was forced to act as the victim's servant for a period of two years.

5. A man was found drunk leaving a tavern and disturbing the peace. This was his third offense. He had already been forced to see a minister and had been once reproved publicly in court.
   Punishment: Twelve hours in the stocks.

6. In Virginia a man was found guilty of severely criticizing the governor in explicit terms.
   Punishment: He had his arms broken, his tongue bored through with an awl, was forced to walk a gauntlet of 40 soldiers, and then was banished from the fort. He was also expected to pay 200 pounds.

7. Massachusetts Bay, 1642. Three men were found guilty of raping a nine-year-old girl.
   Punishment: One man was forced to pay a fine and had his nostril slit and seared. He was forced to wear a rope around his neck for 10 years. The other two were fined and whipped.

8. Two minister's sons, students at Harvard, were found guilty of burglary. They were caught in the act.
   Punishment: Whipping.

9. In Boston a man was found guilty of kissing his wife on the Sabbath Day in public. He had returned home after being gone on a sailing voyage for the past three years.
   Punishment: Two hours in the stocks.

Below are several topics that students can investigate. Some will require traditional book-type investigation while others will require a more nontraditional approach such as interviewing people. As students select these topics or as they are assigned, be sure to discuss what type of investigation procedures will work best. These topics lend themselves to cooperative group investigations followed by class presentations.

1. What does it take to become a judge? Find out what training is needed to become a municipal judge today. In addition try to find out what character traits judges believe are needed to be successful as a judge.

2. What kinds of courts exist today and what are their functions? We have many different kinds of courts from mayor's courts to the Supreme Court. Find out what these courts are, what kinds of cases each hears, and their relationship to one another. Prepare a chart to illustrate the relationship between some of them.

3. A man who acts as his own lawyer is said to have a fool for a client. Today lawyers are as abundant as members of any profession. Find out what different kinds of lawyers there are. Then investigate what a person has to do to become a lawyer. What do lawyers have to do to remain current in their profession?

4. The laws of the colonies are drastically different from the laws of today. Investigate some other period in our country's history, such as the Old West, and find out what kind of laws existed and how justice was dispensed.

5. What rules would students like to see implemented and enforced in your school that do not exist now? Take a survey and gather information on problems that students in your school think exist along with a "just" punishment to go with each offense. If you are in an elementary school, you might want to limit the survey to just primary age students. They have a very different perspective on what is fair.

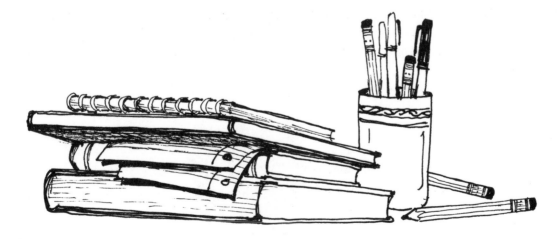

CHAPTER TEN

Colonial Crafts

Art and Necessity

Today, when someone mentions the word *craft,* we get the image of a country-style piece of art that people make or buy and display on a coffee table or hang above a doorway. In colonial America crafts were not just works of art. Indeed, few of them were. For colonists crafts were skills that were regularly utilized to provide things they and their family needed on a daily or seasonal basis. Many of today's "art" crafts were colonial necessities.

This chapter is composed of instructions on how to make things that were used by the colonists in their everyday lives. In some cases the procedure mirrors what the colonists would do. In other cases it adapts modern technology so that students can produce a product similar to what the colonists made. All of the projects are designed to be made by students in a classroom, but this does not preclude handing out instructions and inviting students to make them at home. The procedure recommended for each craft can be altered to fit your situation. It may involve setting up a center and allowing students to work in small groups or individually, or it may have you leading the class in the making of the object. Time constraints and materials are all listed. Where possible, historical information that you can pass on to students is given about the craft. By engaging in these hands-on activities students will be able to understand more clearly what life as a colonist was like.

Like people today the colonists had to have light at night. In the winter dawn came late and dusk was early. That left plenty of time to do things in the home during dark hours. Candles, which today might add an aesthetic atmosphere to an intimate dinner, were merely light needed to eat supper for the colonists. Candles were both common and valued in the colonial household because like today's electric lamp they were a necessity.

In the early days of the colonies candles were made by the woman in the household. As the children became old enough to work (for candle dipping that would have been about five), they helped. By the eighteenth century candles were being made and sold in cities by a craftsman called a chandler. The well-to-do might be able to buy their candles, but most people still had to make them.

Since candle molds were expensive, the dipping method was used by most colonists. This process, though not requiring a great deal of strength or knowledge, did require time. It was not practical for a woman to set everything up to make only a dozen candles since a household needed several hundred candles to make it through the year. Consequently, candle dipping was usually done once a year. Autumn or late summer was the preferred time for several reasons. First, it was when the bayberry became ripe for picking. This waxy berry created a superior scented candle all the colonists wanted. Second, colonists needed to pick a day that was not so cold that this work could not be done outdoors. The common material for candle making was tallow made from the fat of an animal. The stench created from boiling the fat (some of which was rancid from being saved for a while) required that this be done outdoors. If the candles were made indoors, everyone who could find an excuse to go outside did so. Third, candle dipping required cooler temperatures so that the wax could solidify on the candle. For that reason a cool autumn day was best, although autumn was so full of harvesting and other jobs it was not always the most convenient time. Because 100 candles could be made on a cool day, several days were usually set aside for this task.

Besides tallow and bayberry, beeswax was also used. Unlike tallow which produced an odor and smoked when it burned, beeswax and bayberry burned cleaner and brighter. It took thousands of berries to make just one candle, making the bayberry quite valuable. In fact, a fine was levied in some colonies for picking bayberries before they were ripe. The wick was usually made of string made from a plant. Thicker wicks meant brighter candles. Ben Franklin learned that by putting two wicks in a candle he could get a brighter light to accommodate his nightly writing.

ACTIVITY *Candle Dipping*

The procedure below accommodates a full class of students. Modern candle making procedure recommends an assortment of materials and ingredients designed to produce a bright, long-lasting candle. The recipe and procedure below will produce a usable candle that burns quickly and has less than optimum light. The dipping process, however, is the experience that students will enjoy, and hopefully it will allow them to better realize the tedious work the colonists faced in producing light for their homes.

The trick to this procedure is in the preparation. Getting the wax melted and setting up the stations will make the actual dipping easy. The dipping can easily be done in one class period of 45 minutes.

Materials:

1. paraffin (five pounds is enough for a class of 25)–Paraffin is inexpensive and can be bought at hobby shops and at supermarkets.
2. old crayons for coloring
3. two or three coffee cans for melting the wax
4. hot plate or stove
5. double boiler (preferred) or a pot with water
6. One to three sets of soup or vegetable cans with six cans in a set. You will be setting up stations at which 8 to 10 students will work.
7. wick material–This can be bought or you can use a very thin twine. The wick should be made of a natural material. Twine will probably smoke and leave a black ash. Prepared wick is treated to prevent this.
8. water
9. pencils or sticks (one per student)
10. warming tray (optional)

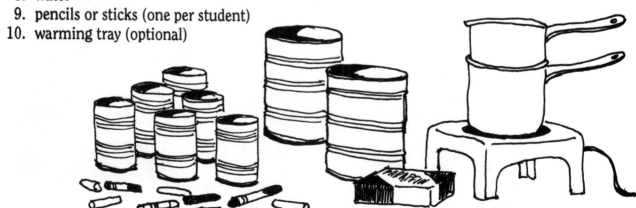

Procedure:

1. Melt the paraffin by breaking it up into small pieces and putting it in the coffee cans. It is safer to melt the wax in a double boiler or in a pot filled with boiling water. This prevents the wax from getting too hot and even igniting.

2. While the wax is melting, set up one to three stations for dipping. Each station can accommodate up to 10 students.
   – A table or set of desks arranged to form a table is needed.
   – Cover the table with newspaper.
   – Each station will use six vegetable or soup cans.

3. Have students prepare wicks for dipping. (This can be done a day ahead of time or for homework.) Do this by tying a six to eight inch piece of wick to a stick or pencil. The piece of wick that hangs downs should be a little longer than the soup or vegetable cans at the stations.

4. Pour wax into three cans per station. Students can vote on the colors they want. Melt the crayons in the smaller cans with wax to give each can of melted wax a color. Colors should be compatible (yellows and reds or blues and purples) so that as the wax layers with every dip the resulting candle is not just a dirty gray color.

5. Fill the remaining cans with cold water. Some colonists used warm water instead of cold water. When the candles were dipped from the wax into warm water the resulting layer had microscopic pockets of oxygen in them. This caused the candle to burn brighter. The process is called "feathering."

6. Arrange the cans at each station alternating between cans with wax and cans with water. The wax will begin cooling as soon as it is off the heat source. Therefore, you may find yourself reheating the wax at each station. To avoid this inconvenience you can put the cans on a warming tray at each station to slow the cooling process.

7. Have students at each station move around the table dipping their wick first in a wax can and then in a water can. Tell them *not* to hold the wick in the hot wax too long or it will melt the wax that has already accumulated on the wick. A two-second dip is all that is needed. If wax splashes or drips on a body part, it may startle students but will not hurt them.

8. About 15 to 20 dips will result in a satisfactory candle. These candles will be soft and pliable. If students want to shape or etch a design in them after all dipping is done, they can.

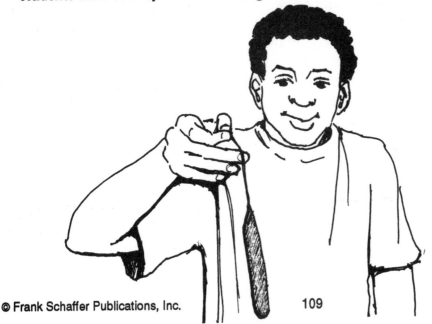

VARIATION *Making Candle Molds*

Tin molds were soon being sold by peddlers in the colonies. These molds allowed the colonist to pour the melted wax or tallow directly into the mold. What a time saver! Eight, twelve, or sixteen candles could be made at a time.

These molded candles did not burn as well as the dipped candles. The wax was more compact and thus burned less brightly. Still, the convenience outweighed the inferior product and many colonists preferred this method to the dipping.

Materials:

1. paraffin–one pound of paraffin will make several small can candles. You may want to supplement this wax supply by getting students to bring in old candle pieces to melt down.
2. wick material–as described in candle dipping
3. candle molds–This is where you and your students can get creative. You will need small objects which can be used as molds. Possibilities include ice cube trays, small juice cans, small milk cartons used in schools, and tuna cans.
4. old crayons for coloring
5. one or two coffee cans for melting the wax
6. hot plate or stove
7. double boiler (preferred) or a pot with water
8. water
9. pencils or sticks (one per student)
10. cooking oil
11. nail or metal washer

Procedure:

1. Melt wax as described in candle dipping but color it with melted crayons. Students can decide on the color.
2. Wash out the candle mold and oil the inside of it.
3. Tie the wicking string to the nail or washer and lay it in the center of the mold. Tie the top of the wick to a pencil or stick and lay it across the top of the mold.
4. Pour in the melted wax nearly to the top. As the paraffin cools, it will shrink so that the final candle will not be as big as the mold. Allow it to cool overnight.
5. Remove the candle from the mold by turning it upside down and tapping lightly. If it is stubborn, you may need to dip the whole mold briefly in hot water to loosen it. Clip the wick to a desired length.

Colonial Storage Chests With Pennsylvania German Design

Storage space was at a premium in most colonial homes, especially the smaller salt-box houses of the early colonial period. Dinnerware, linen, tools, and just about everything had to be stored during the day when the family was using the single room house for daily work. The chest was an important piece of furniture. Chests came in many sizes having been made individually by numerous craftsmen. Some were the size of the old steamer chests and could double for chairs. Others were small, holding deeds and documents.

By the eighteenth century some of the best chests were being made by the Pennsylvania German furniture makers (known also as the Pennsylvania Dutch). On each article they would paint small designs and pictures depicting objects reminiscent of their European heritage and eventually of their new home in America. Certain designs became standard such as the tulip, a heart, or a geometrical design so that today we recognize these decorations as Pennsylvania Dutch objects.

ACTIVITY   *Making Colonial Storage Chests*

The activity below allows students to create their own small chests in which they can keep special treasures. The focus of the activity is on the design they paint on the chest. It can be done in two class periods. One period is needed to prepare the box and practice the designs. The second period is needed for drawing and painting the design. It would be a good idea to prepare a demonstration model yourself so that students can get an idea of what the finished product will look like.

Materials:
a sturdy box–The box should have a lid like a shoe box, candy box, or cigar box.
poster paints–The colors that were typical for the Pennsylvania Germans included tan, light and dark green, dark red, and brown. You may want to have students experiment mixing colors to arrive at the colors you want.
paintbrushes of different sizes
black felt tip marker
water and small bowls for cleaning brushes during painting

Procedure:
1. The first day paint the entire box with tan or light green poster paint so that all printing is hidden. Allow the boxes to dry overnight.
2. Also this first day hand out or post a copy of the Pennsylvania German designs featured on the following pages. Allow students time to practice drawing these designs with the felt tip marker and plan how they want to use them in the decorating of their chests.
3. On the second day have students draw the designs on their boxes with pencil. They can then go over the pencil outlines with markers. They can use other colored paints to fill in the drawings. Allow them to dry overnight.

Designs of the Pennsylvanian Germans

These two pages contain designs that were frequently used by the Pennsylvania Germans (often called the Pennsylvania Dutch) in decorating chests and other pieces of furniture. Many of these symbols are traditional, and their use goes back to when these people were living in Germany. They brought these designs with them to America during the Colonial Period and then each craftsman made changes and added new designs as time went on. As you use these designs as your models, you may want to make small changes of your own.

113

FS-10139 Life As a Colonist

Drying Fruits and Vegetables

A very important part of the colonial experience was the act of preparing food for the winter. There were no refrigerators or ice chests. Occasionally a colonist could put leftover meat in a crock and place the crock in a nearby stream to keep it cooled. Root cellars could also be dug. Food stored below the ground would stay cooler much the same as our basements today are cooler than any other level of the house.

Every colonist, however, had to prepare for the long winter and try to avoid the "starving time" during the last days of that season. That meant that everything had to be either dried, pickled, or salted. The Indians taught the first colonists how to sun dry their fruits and vegetables. Students can dry their own fruits and vegetables to experience what it was like. They will also come to appreciate what the colonists went through during a hard winter when the only thing they had to eat was what they had dried and saved the previous autumn.

ACTIVITY   *Drying Fruits and Vegetables*

The processes below are not guaranteed. The age of the fruits and vegetables that you use can affect how well they dry. Try to dry as many different varieties as you can so that students can see which ones might have been more successful for colonists and which ones were the most work. For best results use a sunny location to do the drying. If that means putting them outside, be sure to cover them with cheesecloth to avoid contamination by insects. Bring them in at night if the process takes longer than one day.

Materials:
cheesecloth
heavy thread and needle
wire cooling tray
clean, white cloth
coat hangers
knives for peeling and pairing

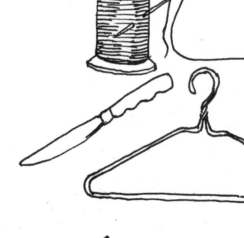

Fruits and Vegetables to Dry:

peas

hot peppers

corn

green beans

tomatoes (small cherry
   tomatoes work best)

pears

apples

grapes

peaches

apricots

FS-10139 Life As a Colonist

Drying Fruits and Vegetables (continued)

General Guidelines:

The water content of the fruit or vegetable as well as the temperature, amount of sunlight, and humidity will affect the length of time it takes to dry any of the foods. Plan on six hours or longer for vegetables since they tend to have a lower water content. Fruits will take at least eight hours and probably longer for the the really juicy ones like peaches.

You will know that the vegetables are done when they feel hard or brittle. Fruits never attain that degree of dryness. They will feel leathery and may even be slightly moist on the inside.

Drying Fruits:

1. For all fruits except grapes peel, core or pit, and then slice the fruit into pieces about 1/2 inch thick.
2. Apples and pears can be strung using the needle and thread and then hung on a coat hanger in the sun to dry. You can also lay any of the above fruits on the clean cloth in the sun to dry. Cover the fruits with cheesecloth to protect them.
3. Grapes should be washed and laid on the cloth to dry. Grapes take longer since the peel holds the moisture longer.

Note: If you are concerned about germs, heat the dried fruits in the oven at 250° for five minutes.

Drying Vegetables:

1. Corn should be husked and the kernels cut from the cob. Dry these on a clean sheet in the sun.
2. Peas should be shelled and also dried on the clean sheet in the sun. The hulls will crack and can be removed when they are dry.
3. Beans and hot peppers can be washed and then strung on thread. Hang the strings from a coat hanger. Unlike the other fruits and vegetables, they dry best in a warm, shaded place such as an attic.
4. Tomatoes (actually a fruit) should be put on the clean sheet to dry. Like grapes, they will take awhile.

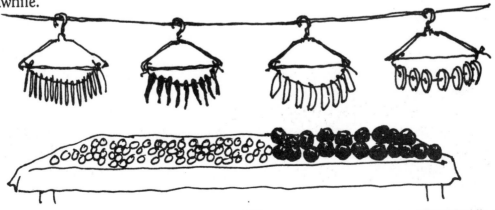

Drying Fruits and Vegetables (continued)

Storage:

When any of the fruits and vegetables are dried, you should plan on storing them. The colonists would have put them in crocks and covered them. They needed to be in a place safe from critters that would be looking for a meal.

You can use sealable plastic containers. The temptation will be to try eating some of the dried foods immediately, but the real lesson is to save the fruits and vegetables for a month or two and then use them just as the colonists would. Label all containers and put the date on them showing when they were stored. Store them in a dry place since too much moisture could spoil them.

Reusing Dried Fruits and Vegetables:

There are two basic ways that dried foods can be eaten. First, they can be eaten as is. The fruits are especially good this way and many students already have experienced eating dried fruits in trail mix forms. Below is a recipe for just such a treat.

Ingredients:
dried apples, apricots, pears, grapes (raisins), and peaches
nuts
honey
powdered sugar

Procedure:
1. Chop or grind the dried fruit.
2. Mix the fruit and nuts together.
3. Add honey and mix.
4. Make teaspoon-sized balls and roll them in powdered sugar.

The other way of using the dried foods is to cook them. This was the way the colonists used them.

Procedure:
1. Soak the dried fruits or vegetables in boiling water.
2. Let stand two to four hours to let the food soak up the water. Fruits take longer than vegetables.
3. These fruits and vegetables are then ready to be cooked and eaten. They are not appealing after soaking and, therefore, need to be used in a recipe. The apples could become part of the apple fritter recipe in this book.

LITERATURE FOR STUDENTS

Reading can be integrated with any unit on colonial America. The books listed below include literature that is both fiction and nonfiction. The average reading levels are appropriate for middle school students. They are listed alphabetically by title. When possible phone numbers of publishing companies or ISBN numbers are listed.

Nonfiction

1. *Arts and Sciences: A Sourcebook on Colonial America* by Carter Smith. This is one of a series by Carter Smith on many aspects of colonial life. Most are library editions. (203) 740-2220.
2. *Colonial Living* by Edwin Tunis. HarperCollins Children's Books. (800) 242-7737.
3. *Colonial Crafts for You to Make* by Janet and Alex D'Amato. Julian Messner subsidiary of Simon Schuster.
4. *How the Colonists Lived* by Arnold Madison. David McKay Company, Inc., a division of Random House. (800) 733-3000.
4. *A Museum of Early American Tools* by Eric Sloane. Funk and Wagnalls.
5. *Planters, Pilgrims and Puritans* by Richard Tames. Trafalgar Square. (800) 423-4525.
6. *Slumps, Grunts and Snickerdoodles: What Colonial America Ate and Why* by Lila Pearl. Seabury Press. ISBN 0-8164-3152-3.

Historical Fiction

1. *Amos Fortune: Free Man* by Elizabeth Yates. E.P. Dutton and Company. (212) 366-2000.
2. *A Break with Charity: A Story About the Salem Witch Trials* by Ann Rinaldi. Gulliver Books, a subsidiary of Harcourt, Brace Jovanovich.
3. *Light in the Forest* by Conrad Richter. Bantam, Doubleday and Dell. (800) 223-5780.
4. *My Name Is Not Angelica* by Scott O'Dell. Dell Publishing, 1989. ISBN 0-440-40379-0.
5. *The Primrose Way* by Jackie French Koller. Harcourt, Brace Jovanovich. (800) 346-8648.
6. *The Village Life in Colonial Times* by James E. Knight. Troll Associates. (800) 526-5289. This is one of a series by James Knight. All of the books focus on some aspect of colonial life within the context of a story.
7. *The Witch of Blackbird Pond* by Elizabeth George Speare. Bantam, Doubleday, Dell. (800) 223-5780.

Biography

1. *Ann Hutchinson* by Elizabeth Ilgenfritz. Chelsea House Publishers, a division of Mainline Books. (800) 848-2665.
2. *The Many Lives of Benjamin Franklin* by Mary Pope Osborne. Dial Press. (212) 366-2000.

COMPUTER PROGRAMS ON COLONIAL AMERICA

Below is a listing of computer software that can be integrated with the study of colonial life in America. Some of the software deals with the colonial time period exclusively while others only contain historical references to it. Included with each entry is the title, publishing company, computer format, and a brief synopsis. Computer format abbreviations are:

Apple II–software that runs on Apple II with a 5.25" drive
Apple IIGs–software that runs on the Apple II-GS with a 3.5" drive
PC–software that runs on MS/DOS with 5.25" drive
PC 3.5–software that runs on MS/DOS with a 3.5" drive
MAC–software that runs on a Macintosh Computer
CD-ROM–Compact Disk-Read Only Memory software

1. *Conversations With Great Americans*: *A Young America*. Focus Media. Apple II. Students play reporter and interview famous people from America's early years.

2. *Decisions, Decisions*: *Colonization*. Tom Snyder Productions. Apple II, MAC, PC, PC 3.5. This program allows students to apply what they learned about American colonization to colonization efforts in a space setting.

3. *The Great American History Knowledge Race*. Focus Media. Apple II, PC, PC 3.5 in lab packs. A great review tool in a game format. Students capture different categories including a category on colonial America.

4. *Pilgrim Quest*. Ellen Nelson Learning Library published by Decision Development Corporation. PC 3.5, PC/CD-ROM, MAC. This simulation has students make decisions similar to those that the Pilgrims faced in order to survive. Includes much historical reference.

5. *Revolution '76*. Compton's Newmedia. Apple IIGS, PC, PC 3.5. Students make political and economic decisions in this interactive simulation that allows them to use their knowledge of the Colonial Period to make decisions regarding the American Revolution.

6. *Time Tunnel*: *Early America*. Focus Media. Apple II, PC, PC 3.5 in lab packs. Students identify famous people from America's early years.

7. *Timeliner Data Disk*: *American History*. Tom Snyder Productions Apple II, PC. Includes all time lines in American history including the Colonial Era. Also available for MAC under the title *MacTimeliner Data Disk*: *American History*.

RESOURCES FOR TEACHERS

The print resources listed below will provide you, the teacher, with additional information on living conditions and lifestyle during the Colonial Period in American history. Most of the sources can be found in a public library or a college library. If the book has an ISBN number, it is listed. This will enable you to reference the book in any bookstore.

Creekmore, Betsey B. *Traditional American Crafts*. Hearthside Press Inc., 1968.

Demos, John. *A Little Commonwealth*. Oxford University Press, 1970.

Ewen, David. *Songs of America*. Greenwood Press, 1978. ISBN 0-313-20166-3.

Hawke, David Freeman. *Everyday Life in Early America*. Harper & Row, Publishers, 1988. ISBN 0-06-091251-0.

Hoople, Cheryl G. *The Heritage Sampler: A Book of Colonial Arts and Crafts*. The Dial Press, 1975. ISBN 0-8037-5414-0.

Langdon, William Chauncy. *Everday Things in American Life*. Charles Scribner & Sons, 1937.

Miller, John C. *First Frontier: Life in Colonial America*. University Press of America, 1966. ISBN 0-8191-4878-4.

Pearl, Lila. *Slumps, Grunts and Snickerdoodles: What Colonial America Ate and Why*. Seabury Press, 1975. ISBN 0-8164-3152-3.

Reich, Jerome R. *Colonial America*. Prentice Hall, 1989. ISBN 0-13-151176-9.

Shryock, Richard Harrison. *Medicine and Society in America: 1660-1860*. Cornell University Press, 1960.

Sloane, Eric. *A Museum of Early American Tools*. Funk and Wagnalls, 1964.

Wendorff, Ruth. *Cornhusk Dolls*. Arco Publishing Co., 1975. ISBN 0-668-02883-1.

AN INDEX OF ACTIVITIES

The index found on the following pages is a guide to student activities developed for each chapter. This index is designed to act as a quick reference for finding a specific activity. It is also intended to be a planning guide by providing a list of subjects and skills that each activity involves. Most of the categories are self-explanatory. Additional notes are included below.

"Art" relates to all activities that allow students to design, draw, diagram, or develop something visual. Bulletin board and craft activities are all labeled with the AR symbol.

"Critical Thinking" involves skills such as evaluating, productive thinking, planning, and decision making.

"Cooking" as well as some "Art" activities have a "Math" label since measuring is a part of the process.

"Researching" relates to any activity that has students participating in traditional research such as using reference material as well as nontraditional research such as interviewing or observing.

"Speaking/Listening" is identified for all activities that have students presenting information to the class, discussing information in a group, or contacting outside sources in an interview.

As you use the activities, you may find yourself changing them to fit your specific plans. As you do, you will find that new skills and subjects will be incorporated into each activity. Below is the key to all abbreviations used in this index.

AR = Art
CO = Cooking
CT = Critical Thinking
SL = Speaking/Listening
HE = Health
MA = Math
RE = Research
SC = Science
SS = Social Studies
WR = Writing
 * = denotes activities that include
        reproducible student pages

CHAPTER-BY-CHAPTER ACTIVITY INDEX

Chapter Six – Colonial Education

Chapter Seven – Health and Medicine

Chapter Eight – Recreation, Sports, and Holidays

Chapter Nine – Crime and Punishment in the Colonies

Chapter Ten – Colonial Crafts